The Heart of Hope

THE *Heart* OF *Hope*

Contemplating Life, Awakening Love

Michael Downey

Pauline
BOOKS & MEDIA
Boston

Library of Congress Cataloging-in-Publication Data

Downey, Michael.
  The heart of hope : contemplating life, awakening love /
Michael Downey.
     p. cm.
  ISBN 0-8198-3388-6

  1. Downey, Michael. 2. Meditations. 3. Downey, Michael—
Travel—Vietnam. 4. Vietnam—Description and travel. I. Title.
  BX2182.3.D69 2005
  242—dc22

                          2004029050

Cover design by Rosana Usselmann
Cover photos by Inmagine and Istockphoto
Calligraphy by Duy Cuong, an artist in Cantho, Vietnam

"P" and PAULINE are registered trademarks of the Daughters of
St. Paul

Published by Pauline Books & Media, 50 Saint Pauls Avenue,
Boston, MA 02130-3491.

Printed in U.S.A.

www.pauline.org

Pauline Books & Media is the publishing house of the
Daughters of St. Paul, an international congregation of women
religious serving the Church with the communications media.

1 2 3 4 5 6 7 8 9   11 10 09 08 07 06 05

Table of Contents

Introduction

There is a story told of a mother and her little daughter in Trinidad. They are the poor of the earth, and the mother takes great care each evening to launder the one well-worn dress that her daughter wears to school day after day. Each morning, as the little girl leaves the front door to set off for class, her mother asks her to stop and turn toward her for a moment. "Just stand there. I love to look at you."

Contemplation is a way of looking, a way of seeing. The more I see, the more I love. And the more I love, the more I see. Seeing by loving; loving by seeing. But the one caught up in contemplation knows that it is not only I who look and gaze and behold; it is the Other, whose name above all naming is Love, who gazes upon me. A beloved child hears the words of a mother: "Just stand there. I love to look at you." It is ours to be gazed upon...even while gazing.

This little book is about looking and seeing. In January 2004, I visited Vietnam for the first time. Upon my return, I could not but savor all that had happened to me there, in that place of sight and sound, of heart and hunger, of suffering and hope, of scent and spirit and Spirit. For me, the visit was the occasion for an *awakening of the heart.* And upon waking, or being awakened, the eyes are the first to open: to see again, as if for the first time; to look with the eyes of the heart. What I saw there, what happened to me amidst the places and among the people of Vietnam, I have tried to express in "The Hope of a World in One Smile," the central reflection in this volume.

The essay was too long to find publication in a periodical or journal of spirituality. But I was unwilling to cut it into parts or shave half the pages away, for every movement of this heart was a vital part of the story. The reflection found its way to one publisher who judged that it should be sent to a secular magazine so that it might receive a wider readership. Another publisher urged me to develop the theological insights underpinning the story, a task I took up in earnest. But as I tried to tease out the theology at the story's heart, my voice became that of an academic theologian rather than that of a spiritual writer or teacher in the ways of the heart. The central story and the theological reflections were, as the Irish put it, "like chalk and cheese."

Aware that the writings of the Vietnamese Cardinal Francis Xavier Nguyen Van Thuan, published by Pauline Books and Media, have a wide readership in English, and having had several fruitful exchanges with the Daughters of Saint Paul over the last years, I sent "The Hope of a World in One Smile" to them for their consideration. From the first, Madonna Therese Ratliff, FSP, was able to see what I saw, and helped me find a way to say it. She recognized images, the pictures at play in my experience of Vietnam, and helped me name them. "What do you see?" I asked her. "A face." Then: "Hands. Bowing. Eating. Dress. Sea. Bridge. Teacher. Heart." In that instant, I knew that I had found an editor who understood, someone who is able to look and see and say as I do. She cared for each word on every page. My gratitude to her is beyond measure.

What follows the central story, then, is a series of "image reflections," each image emerging from "The Hope of a World in One Smile." They are related to the story in the way that the slimmer, side panels of an iconostasis are related to the central panel, always leading the eye back to the center, even as each panel can stand alone, offering its own meaning and message.

One by one, the image reflections convey insight about a core feature of the Christian spiritual life: faith and forgiveness, suffering and hope, care for the body and for the poor of the earth, the costliness of fidelity, being rooted in a tradition, grief and gratitude, the need for good teaching and direction, the in-breaking of grace in the face of the other. While not in any way a comprehensive treatment of the Christian spiritual life, the insights that emerge from the image reflections may again be likened to the iconostasis in that the features of the spiritual life treated here are all related to one another, but draw us back to the center: Being conformed to the person of Christ, brought into communion with one another and every living creature in the gift of the Spirit, to the glory of God the Father. Pausing for a moment before each image, standing still, we might see the movement of God at the heart of reality and hear the movements of God in the beating of the human heart. The image reflections are an exercise in a spirituality of seeing, a contemplative spirituality of beholding in the face of ordinary people and events, the shimmering of hope that is so often in such short supply among peoples of plenty.

In step with Vietnamese custom, I was given a new name shortly after my arrival there. To be called *Thay Tam,* Teacher of the Heart, has provided occasion for me to look back with gratitude over my twenty-five years of teaching. Whatever the subject matter at hand, it has always been *the heart* that I have sought to educate in my students. Naming three of these students here is testimony to the truth that it is this teacher who has so much yet to learn—especially in the ways of the heart. And so, for what I have learned from each of them while at Saint John's Seminary, Camarillo, I express my heartfelt thanks: to Eugene Justin Lee, who first opened

Asia's door to me; to Francis Aytona Mendoza, my student assistant over several years, a living testimony to the buoyancy and endurance of the people of the Philippines; to Bao Quoc Thai: his life, his people, and his homeland awakened *The Heart of Hope.*

Michael Downey
Thay Tam

November 1, 2004
All Saints

Part One

The Hope of a World
in One Smile

☞ The heart longs. In its longing, it laces itself 'round. This is the way of the heart. At times it is laced 'round by another. Even when laced with another in love, the heart can get weary, washed out. On its own, it can tire more quickly. Either way, it can lose its way. The heart's love can become locked in on itself or it can become a handcuffed heart whose love promised freedom but delivered fetters instead. Even the noblest of fetters bind. What loosens the heart to love after it has been locked up? Laced, lone, or locked, the heart gets another chance sometimes. And if it dares, the heart can learn once again how to love with a love that wants *only* to love, with a love the pushes out into the vastness of an ever-widening, never-ever-to-be-exhausted generosity.

It was in Vietnam that I learned that my heart could fall in love again, more deeply than ever before. Not with another, but with a people and a land.

🖎   Long before beginning the first grade, perhaps at the age of three, maybe four, I learned about missionaries going to foreign lands. I can still remember a leaflet left in the pews of my parish, Most Blessed Sacrament Church, with photos of the Belgian priest Damien of Molokai, Missionary to the Lepers. Two photos set alongside one another: the youthful, dark-haired, and good-looking Father Damien, white-robed and newly ordained; then Damien the Leper: boils on his face, disease-darkened skin in a torn and tattered black hat and tunic. Later, as we sat obediently at our desks in Blessed Sacrament School, there were always pictures of malnourished children and their parents, visually pleading with us from places in the Far East and Southeast Asia.

❧ Digging now from this storehouse of memory, I unearth the innocent desire of a not-so-very-devout boy in urban Philadelphia to go to one of these places. And, for reasons as mysterious as the allure itself, to go to Vietnam as a missionary, to *that* place and *those* people, just as Thérèse of Lisieux wanted to go. Perhaps I felt a connection with her. It seemed as unlikely for me—an Irish Catholic schoolboy on the eastern seaboard of the United States of America—to get to Saigon as it did for Thérèse, the young Carmelite enclosed in a strict monastery in French Normandy. But as her desire was real and deep, so was mine. In my childhood I dreamed of going to Vietnam, to die with the Vietnamese, for them, for love of them.

❧ Dreams of childhood fade in the press of practicality. The heart is numbed by the onslaught of words and images that promise more than they deliver. But in the depth of dream or in the glimpse of a child all wonder-eyed, our hearts beat for eternal life, the life that comes from God as gift, a gift we can barely imagine: a life of sheer aliveness; living with, and in, and from Love itself. Most days we breathe the air of a subtle anesthesia, half-awake to the wonder of abundant life around us, convinced with the likes of Jack Nicholson that this is "as good as it gets." But it can be supremely better for those who are willing to go deep, to be plunged into a Love as wide and deep and hot and cool and blue and green and purple as to be beyond any measure or calculation. And to be carried by Love, indeed buoyed up by Love itself—from here to a there, which is no *where*.

℘   The story of this heart falling in love again begins in May 1997, in Camarillo, California. Saint John's Seminary was already empty of most students and faculty. The place was all mine to set up a new office in tranquility. No matter how promising a new opportunity might be, the task of setting up house and getting installed in a new workplace is sheer drudgery. I was carrying a deep tiredness, a cumulative exhaustion, a massive sleep debt not unlike what so many of us carry through life. Our bodies weary, our spirits sag, our hearts are heavy from so much of what we carry: disappointment, resentment, frustration, hurt, uncertainty, feeling misunderstood, unappreciated. When a heavy heart is laden with layers of sludge and silt, we long for purity of heart, a clean heart, a heart free of darkness, a heart that is lit and light with love.

I shall always remember that he was the first student I met there: Dominique Thuan Pham. Grinning, he shyly approached with a gentle and quiet bow, extending both hands to take mine: "My name is Thuan Pham. You don't know me. But you've probably heard about me. I'm one of the boat people. I came over here from Vietnam." Only later did I learn that he and members of his family had made more than a dozen failed attempts to leave Vietnam. But here he was, safe and secure, with another dream in his heart. Surrounded and sustained by friends and family, his face was as fresh as a newly done good deed. Two brown eyes, so deep they were black, held all the promise that only a lifetime of struggle can imagine.

Celebrating Vietnamese New Year at the seminary for the first time, Thuan was there. Radiant in their *ao dai,* Vietnamese Catholics came from the far reaches of Southern California to Los Angeles— "Los," as they call this land of never-ending sunshine and eternal traffic—to celebrate the happiest time of year: *Tet,* Lunar New Year, the time to venerate ancestors and to express hope for prosperity, luck, and longevity. Trees adorned with *li xi,* lucky money, in red and golden envelops, were carefully propped up in dining room and chapel. All around the place, native costumes in shimmering blue and gold and turquoise draped thin-as-a-wick figures; silky black hair of women and young girls held tightly in place by the corona-like *khan dong.* All so svelte. *It must be the rice,* I thought.

℘ It was not all that long before his hair was gone. Thuan's. Chemotherapy robbed him of that black silky mop, taken away from him by the hope of a healthy life—one free of the death-dealing tumor eating away at his brain. The nervous grin remained as he stared out from beneath a deepness deeper than the sea he had tried so often to cross—and finally did—to the land of promise. I wondered if he wondered as I wondered: All that way...for this?

The last time I saw him was when I went to his deathbed to keep an hour-long afternoon vigil with Ed, one of Thuan's seminary professors who stood by him and the family through every one of those terrible days. Thuan was sleeping. And he was dying. Ed drew near him while I looked on and whispered an "Our Father," "Hail Mary," and "Glory Be."

We three were together again just weeks later when Ed put Thuan into the earth and asked God to take him to eternal life, to comfort a family—mother and father and sisters and brother—who had left their home for freedom, and now so deeply grieved as they stood shoulder to shoulder on the land they once dreamed of as heaven. Ed, now a bishop, believes with all his heart that Thuan looks down on him from heaven. And prays for him.

℞   Bao thought he might have a brain tumor, too. The steady strain of seminary life was weighing: severe headaches about which he did not complain. He wondered and worried quietly that, like Thuan, he too might be taken early in life.

My first impression of Bao remains: sheer joy in living. When the new students came to the seminary in September 1998, Bao Thai, recently arrived in the United States, could hardly make himself understood. But he rose quietly and a little nervously to tell faculty and classmates: "Bao Thai. My name is Bao *(pause)* Thai. Don't worry, if this is hard to remember, just call me 'Bow Tie,'" putting his fingers to his neck in the fashion of straightening a fancy dress tie. He won us immediately.

Bao has a most uncanny feel for idiom and jargon. He learns languages by grasping on to catchy phrases. In the midst of talking through some ideas from his course or struggling with a difficult concept after class, he would suddenly pipe up: "I got it!"—his crisp way of letting me know that he finally understood what I had been laboring to communicate to him and his classmates. For weeks, echoes of "I got it!" punctuated with the gleeful sounds of a tickled chipmunk would be heard in seminary halls and classrooms. This was soon replaced by "I *love* it," describing his life in the seminary, his parish work on weekends, or his extended period of parish internship. Many months later I asked him his favorite of all English sayings. Without a second thought, he blurted out in clearly enunciated tones: "You *freak* me out!" (with decided emphasis on the k).

℘   It was Bao who invited me into another world: Little Saigon in Orange County, California, enclave within enclave of extended families tucked away in the shadows of the freeways of "Los," or shoved in behind the elbows of endless strip malls in Garden Grove and Westminster. Here were driveways and cul-de-sacs jammed with old secondhand Hyundais and Nissans. Small homes, stark and spare, packed to the gills with mothers and fathers, grandparents and aunts and uncles, and more aunts and uncles still, then children—all wrapped in the unmistakable aroma of Asian spices dripping near-visibly through the air. Circles upon circles of people—almond eyes become oval with fascination at the sight of state-of-the-art digital cameras or computers—crowded into sparse kitchens, plastic kiddy chairs everywhere, the living rooms appointed with patio furniture, organizer boxes, storage boxes...and sprays of flowers in nearly every room.

Then at night, layers and layers of children sleeping on floors, bodies laced together for warmth and comfort, all connected by blood and by work and, more, by a common story. Until now, I had only heard about them: the refugees in the proverbial backyard, interlocked in a vast world of immigrant underground, next door to the "Happiest Place on Earth," Orange County's Disneyland. Doing whatever work they can get their hands on, sometimes from their homes, most working hard ten-hour-a-day-jobs if they can find them, they are bonded to one another and to their homeland by a common story of struggle and suffering.

☞   Bao did not speak of his headaches or the seminary strain; it was another story that he wanted to tell me. But it would take me years—and whatever years I might have left—to learn it. My elementary lessons in this story began when Bao requested that I direct his thesis on the spirituality of the Vietnamese martyrs, about which I knew nothing. It was hard work for both of us each day for nearly fifteen months. I became *Su phu nhiet thanh,* Faithful Teacher, and he *De tu trung thanh,* Faithful Student, but the tables began to turn from the first. Never before had I seen such respect and reverence for learning, for education, for study, as I came to see in him. Hungry he came to me, grateful beyond telling for whatever I might have to offer.

The years of hard work reaped rich rewards. Bao Quoc Thai defended his Master's thesis with distinction and was ordained a priest less than two months later. It was only then, during the celebrations of his ordination, that I began to learn the other parts of this story, the chapters that the student dared not tell the teacher—perhaps too painful; perhaps he did not wish to evoke sympathy.

There is the father imprisoned for eight years after the fall of Saigon, wrenched from his wife and five young children and thrown into a "reeducation camp" near the Vietnamese-Chinese border. There is the eldest sister who cared for baby Bao as their mother went to work each day, work that she continues to this day near Little Saigon in Orange County. There are the brothers and sisters uneasily awaiting a mother's return from work at lunchtime. There is bright Bao, who went on to university in Saigon and began teaching high school computer science, but who wanted to be a priest. Bao knew he would be denied admission to the seminary because of the "sins of the father," a Colonel in the South Vietnamese Army before the fall of Saigon, and so Bao never spoke a word of it to anyone. Not ever, at least while he was in Vietnam. Not to his teachers, his family, his closest friend, his pastor.

The more I learned the more I knew that I needed to go. To Vietnam. To the homeland. To that people I had once, as a boy, wanted to die for.

☞ "We go," Bao's way of inviting me to return with him to his homeland. But the SARS epidemic in the Spring of 2003 instilled fear in the hearts of the parents of the newly ordained priest. They were convinced that the Communist government was covering up the extent of SARS in Vietnam. They pleaded with their son to wait a while before returning to Vietnam. Aware of the importance of respect for the elders among the Vietnamese, Faithful Teacher instructed Faithful Student: "Pray every day to Our Lady of La Vang. She will bring us to Vietnam one day." Bao assured a doubting teacher that the delay was God's providence. "Instead, we go to Vietnam for *Tet*. Good Weather. Best time of year." And so we went to ring in the Year of the Monkey, arriving at the Saigon airport in mid-January of 2004.

☞ The first sensation was of being in a swamp surrounded-to-suffocation by dozens and dozens of cardboard boxes tumbling off the conveyor belt in baggage claim, each one carefully labeled and exactly seventy pounds—no more no less—packed to the limit with goods brought back to families and friends by returning *Viet Kieu,* those Vietnamese, despised by the Communist government, who had fled the country in the years since the fall of Saigon. Wading through boxes while dodging push carts on our way to pass customs, by what seemed to me no less than a minor miracle, we gained entry to Communist Vietnam without event.

It was then that I saw them, all of them, every one of them, as if at once. Waves, fields, layers, throngs of bronze, golden people. Shoved behind guarded barricades and already bathed-to-dripping in that close and clammy air of Vietnam's coolest month, arms reaching, stretching, straining, waving in the steamy thickness of the air, holding high bouquets and banners heralding the advent of the Lunar New Year, all basking in a liquid exuberance that embraced their loved ones now returned from exile.

Bouquets in bundles of fours and fives, layer upon layer of garlands 'round necks drenched by the dripping humid air. From all corners, hand fans waved inches from my face, offering the slight comfort of some small breeze to this exhausted traveler. "Take a picture!" "Take a picture!" Another of Bao's best lines, "Take a picture!" rang through the air as the dozens swarmed forward to greet their nephew, cousin, spiritual son, neighbor, lifelong friend, but more, the newly ordained priest, Cha Bao.

☞ That is when it began. Or began to begin again. The unlocking of a heart, a heart ready to be plunged to the very bottom where memory gives way to hope.

It started with a few words: "Take a picture!" "Look!" "Look here!" "Look at me!" "Smile!" But suddenly, what I see in my mind's eye are the forgotten ones, those pictures of faces branded forever on the heart. *Those* people are *this* people. The ones in memory's dusty photo album lodged somewhere

in the remote regions of my ribcage, shelved in a forgotten place in my heart for twenty-five years and
more, now pulled out and laid wide open right
before my eyes. I had not looked since 1975 at those
pictures from my youth, all those faces each day in
the morning newspaper, and then in moving pictures on the nightly news. Conical hats covering
black-hair-in-a-bun toothless women, squat-sitting in
corners stirring pots of hot noodle soup. Limbless,
shirtless, hairless teenage boys scavenging for a bite
in villages with names harder to pronounce than
simple Saigon. Little figures with bamboo poles, balancing buckets on both ends, running. Quick. Fast.
Dark-eyed infants with oval mouths, caverns to be
filled with anything in reach. And white men with
guns and tanks rolling over a people and a land that
would one day outwit them.

☞   Then the fall of Saigon at April's end, 1975.
Arms stretching and straining in the air, all a life's
hope hung on those helicopters come dipping and
plucking from the roof of the American Embassy in
those last minutes, grabbing and snatching only this

one and that one to safety, while so many remain stranded, and hundreds more on the streets of Saigon-become-Ho Chi Minh City that morning at 11:30. Then I saw no more pictures. Until this first new day in Saigon-Ho Chi Minh City.

℘   Fast forward: A fifty-something relic of the '60s that is me standing outside the Saigon Airport, wondering if there is room enough for them in a heart already crammed with yellow-edged snaps of the "American War" in Vietnam, photos from newspapers and newsreels showing the war of my generation, forever etched but until now forgotten in the heart's memory. Flanked on both sides by dozens of glistening golden people, beaming family and friends come some distance to greet me as well as Bao. Still sporting signature '60s blue jeans and T-shirt, a duffle bag weighs in one hand while a backpack nearly bends me double. The other hand cannot stretch wide enough to clutch the three bouquets in crimson and gold given to me—all the assurance I need that whatever small gesture I have come all this way to give will find a home in the hearts of these people.

℞   Nothing could have prepared me for what I would see next. Saigon teeming with people: on motorbikes, mopeds, bicycles, in cyclos, cars, taxis, and on foot—all in the streets. A family of four, sometimes five, zooms by me, sandwiched on a single motorcycle. The delivery boy with a steaming hot bowl of noodle soup in one hand, the other hand bracing the center of the handlebar. A sort of Asian wonder boy, five or six years old, singing even as he holds a half-bowl's worth of rice in his mouth, balancing himself on the handlebars of his daddy's hot motorbike! Nowhere do I see a motorcycle helmet. But there are surgical masks on those who can afford them, or who think it does any good. There appear to be no rules of the road: no right lane, left lane flow of traffic. We are swept up, carried along, in a moving, chaotic, free-for-all pushing any and every way you can to get to where you need to go, a rap-line of cacophony and clutter, randomly punctuated by honking and belching, like those curly Q accents placed here and there over the quirkily-strung words of the tonal language that is Vietnamese.

Fragrant flowers in your face at every turn, mostly yellow during the celebration of *Tet*. Piles and layers and rows of yellow life—human and floral—on every street corner. Sensuous, slim bodies of young women sipping cool drinks, lounging cross-legged to one side of a speeding motorcycle, gripping the spaghetti-thin waists of their boyfriends who gun Suzukis, Hondas, Yamahas with a mix of poise and fury. Wooden vegetable stands guarding entry to noodle soup kitchens, hot bowls of *pho* served for breakfast, lunch, and dinner. *Pho* pots on nearly every street huddled around by dozens of thin bodies squatting less than an inch from the ground, their longer-than-life arms hugging bowls while busy chopsticks work at globs of steaming foot-long rice noodles.

Fruit skins strewn everywhere, like fluttering confetti tossed on New Year's Eve in Times Square. Markets bustling and animal parts I've never heard of, let alone seen, on display: hundreds and hundreds of them stretched out on wooden tables, shoppers nudging at still-bloody flesh, poking at the still-live eyes in pigs' heads to test the freshness.

℘   It happened during that first dark night, somewhere between waking and sleeping on sweat-soaked sheets. They were singing. Some of them, how many I could not know, had been milling around the church yard since just after midnight, joined by others gathering in the church at 4:00 A.M. to ready the day with morning Mass. I could hear the gentle ringing of bells and the rhythmic scuffing of flip-flop sandals circling around the entrance to a shrine—or is it a temple?—not far from the church. There was the rhythmic hush of brooms, circle-sounds of sweeping to ready the way for those who would come and go to pray throughout the day, at church, shrine, or temple.

Random buzzing of motorbikes and swooshing of cyclos somewhere between darkness and light... the siren-like wailing of Vietnamese divas going on and on in neighborhood nightclubs about love and heartache...the never-ending clatter of the streets mixed with predawn chants...all began to blend and soothe rather than startle me. Voices strong and full poured themselves into song long before dawn, belting out the praises of God and stirring up in me the only language I knew how to speak at the edge of awakening on the first full morning: the language of tears, of silent sobbing, the heart's memory unlocked and passing through time's floodgates.

With night's muted purple now poised as if to contemplate its strategy for reentry in soft shades of mauve and lavender at the next day's end, the sounds of a busy day-in-the-making were finally greeted by the kiss of yellow sunlight. Tonight—now morn—the "all" of me is bathed, better *christened,* by the images that greeted my arrival: the smiles of these people—bending low, huddling, squatting so close to the ground—an earthen and earthy people who have taken me to themselves from the first.

It is not their faith that came into focus, though that is part of what drew me. It is their "living-ness," a way of being close to the ground, a heartbeat away from the pulsating earth on which the rest of us would rather stand, trod, and trammel, thinking ourselves somehow above and unrelated to it. Their squat-sitting brings them close to the earth and its ways, reminding me too of where I have come from and where I shall go in the end. This is the place where I belong.

☞ The first point of business that morning: get the American visitor properly dressed for the celebrations honoring the newly ordained Cha Bao and for *Tet*. Against the advice of elders and tour guides, I hopped in boyish abandon on the back of whatever motorcycle was offered, holding tight to Phaolo, then Kiet, then Miss Huong, brushing other motorbikes and pedestrians as we whizzed through Saigon's streets looking for *ao dai* for me. We searched mightily for just the right one. Onlookers giggled as the white-bearded foreigner paraded in the open-air market, first in blue, then in red, then in black, and finally in the yellow *ao dai* that gained the approval of friends and passersby. Although I preferred blue, Bao had his way after whispering to the crowd the nature of the occasion. Only later did I learn why the *ao dai* had to be brilliant golden yellow, rich and regal: I was representing the family of the newly ordained priest. I was standing in for the parents who, because of fear or finance, could not return to their homeland with their son.

❧   Welcomed day by day into an ever-widening circle that embraced and celebrated him, the always-respectful and ever-courteous Bao eventually drew near to whisper that friends and family found it so hard to say "Dr. Downey." They wanted to give me a new name, easier on their lips: "Thay Tam." "What does it mean, Bao?" Very matter-of-factly: "Teacher with a Heart, Brother with a Heart, Heart Teacher, Loving Teacher, Teacher of the Heart. We want to call you Thay Tam. Okay, Thay Tam?"

☙   Then: "Soon we go to see her. We must thank her, Thay Tam."

☙   Phaolo walked shoulder to shoulder with us throughout those days, just as he had walked to school side by side with Bao through Saigon's city streets years before. He was the quiet organizer for all our comings and goings, but the minute he got on the bus, into the back of the car, or on the plane, Phaolo would close his eyes and sleep until arrival at our destination. On waking, he would practice his English in soft, sonorous tones: "My name is Hung Nguyen, Phaolo, Paul, the 'Sleeping Child.'" Like so many in his country, Phaolo had worked hard all year long awaiting the few days of rest and rejuvenation at *Tet*. The "Sleeping Child" evoked from me a sense that the whole country of Vietnam, after so many years of toil and struggle, carries a collective sleep debt, not unlike my own.

Boyhood friends, they were ordained priests just three weeks apart: Phaolo in Saigon-become-Ho Chi Minh; Bao in Little Saigon, Orange County. They wanted to travel together, now as newly ordained priests, to that place where they had never been together so that they might pray to her in gratitude for so much that had been given them. And I needed to go, too, to make good on my promise to thank her for bringing us to Vietnam.

℘ The Shrine of Our Lady of La Vang is in the center of Vietnam, just north of the former capital, the Imperial City of Hue. During a great persecution of Christians from 1798 to1801, some took refuge in the jungle near Quang Tri, growing sick and exhausted, knowing that certain execution awaited them. Then, while a small group of the faithful was at prayer, Mary visited them. The Lady of La Vang offered them consolation, promising to receive their prayers with maternal affection. And so she does to this day.

We approached her outdoor shrine, gathering flowers to set at her feet. There was a quietness that deepened as we drew near. I looked up at the Lady dressed in blue and white *ao dai,* golden corona-like *khan dong* holding back her inky hair, the infant in rosy tunic lifted up in her arms. A quiet held me—no, cradled me—for how long I cannot know even now. What I do know is that she was before me, and that he was at my side: *De tu trung thanh.* She had brought us, Faithful Student and Faithful Teacher, here to this place, to this land, and here we stood together looking up at her. Stillness.

Then, from the steps of the shrine dedicated to this Lady who promised maternal affection: Shush, shush, shush; hush, hush, hush. The soft sounds of ageing, bent-over women sweeping with grassy branches. Dozens of them, milling around the feet of the Lady of La Vang, all with no concern but to sweep, whispering prayers that mesh with the sweeping sounds and pour into my ears like a mother's comfort—hush, hush, hush. Then an echo of ripples on unknown and unnamed rivers, the ebb and flow of lapping white waves of this Mother's milk that had carried him—Thuan—from here to there. All that way...for this? And was it not the same waves that carried Bao and Thay Tam from there to here? For this.

The sea had carried them all from here to there. And us from there to here. For this we have come to give thanks. It is that same sea—its separating distance—that until now had kept me from seeing the faces of a people so close to the ground, the ones ducking and running and hiding from bullets and bombs, only to stand up once again and raise their arms high enough to greet me and extend to me a welcome's garland and three bouquets of crimson and gold, too big to hold in one hand.

Through my eyes, and hers, I gazed long and lovingly on a people raped and scarred by pain and torture and hunger, from one generation to the next, first by their own neighbors, then by the French, and finally by Americans. Then there came a word not my own, a question that made me quiver as it found its way to my hearing alone: "What have we done?" Still, and still by my side, Bao whispered in wonder: "I don't understand. Sometimes when I look at her, she smiles at me. But now she looks so sad. I think maybe she's crying. But I don't know why." My words fell into that sweeping silence, the deep quiet of maternal lament, now just loud enough for the Faithful Student becoming Faithful Teacher to hear: "I know why."

☞   Our travels brought us to all three parts of what was once known as the Asian Pearl. In Central Vietnam, we began in Da Nang, whose bay American troops entered when the United States escalated its efforts, then over the Hai Van Pass to the Imperial City of Hue on the serpentine Perfume River, into the cool womb of the underground river of the Phong Nha caves. In the north, we based in lake-laced Hanoi where the marks of French colonialism still prevail in architecture, in cuisine, in the arrangement of neighborhoods and markets. From Hanoi we traveled by overnight train to mountainous cloud-draped Sapa, home to some of Vietnam's more celebrated indigenous peoples, the Hmong. Then back to Lao Cai at the Chinese border, where the remains of reeducation camps dot the landscape. Forever seared in my memory is the mystic Ha Long Bay, dotted with thousands of moss-covered rocks jutting out from the sea, piercing a heavy, hovering, fog-laden sky.

Everywhere we go, the two newly-ordained priests want to celebrate Mass with our small circle: Miss Huong, Kiet, Sau, Thay Tam, and one or another tour guide who, often non-Catholic, looks on. It's hard to do this in North Vietnam, even on a Sunday. The government monitors churches carefully. Permissions are needed, as they are for the lectures and conferences I give in the south, center, and north. Sometimes approvals are requested; sometimes not. Sometimes they are granted; more often not. So more often than not, I show up without much notice, and groups gather quietly and discreetly in church basements or convent parlors. I speak to them under the cover of night's dark or with the protection of a ruse sagely designed to keep the government away from the building where I am speaking. A lesson learned somewhere during my formative years has served me well on many occasions: it is sometimes easier to ask pardon than permission. Providence or chance, we were never caught. Either because of good fortune or La Vang's maternal care, we escaped government scrutiny.

☞ Months before my departure for Vietnam, one of my students told me that he had once tasted thirty-six different fruits in Central Vietnam alone. I learned quickly that in each place it is a sign of respect and appreciation to sample the local fare: the exotic dragon and breast milk fruits of Central Vietnam (I cannot remember the names of the other thirty-four!), Hue's delicate candies, distinctive crepes, and finely pureed rice and shrimp dishes. And everywhere the most luscious coffee, *ca phe sua da,* a legacy no doubt left by the French. Dark, bittersweet, and slow to drip—but unmistakably Vietnamese when laced with sweetened condensed milk and poured over blocks of ice in plastic mugs.

Journeys are punctuated by eating. Guidebooks advise to ensure providing a lunch stop for bus drivers and tour guides. It is unthinkable for the Vietnamese to work through mealtimes. And after lunch, a little time for rest. *How very... well... French!* I thought. There is no fast food in Vietnam. With very little refrigeration anywhere, each meal is carefully prepared from goods brought daily from the local market, invariably by the women of the house. Eating is never rushed. Long, leisurely conversations at morning, noon, and evening seem to make each meal an occasion. And (and this took some getting used to!), toothpicks passed and used with fierce determination after each meal. As we moved about from place to place, or from table to table, an impression was forming, another picture in the making: A nation of small, yellow-near-bronze, bone-thin people...who love to eat!

☞   On the journey south—fourteen of us in the minivan!—we cross seemingly countless small bridges over rivers and streams en route from Saigon to Cantho, a wet and welcoming place in the heart of the Mekong Delta. Everyone slept in the minivan, save the driver, Thay Tam, and Bao. He began to tell me quietly of summers in his mother's family home in Cantho during the years his father was in the reeducation camp near Lao Cai: "I love numbers. When I was little, we leave Saigon at 4:00 A.M. We arrive at 3: 00 P.M. in Cantho to my mother's family home. Long day for me! I count bridges to pass the hours between Saigon and Cantho when we make the trip on the big bus. Over 100 bridges. So many rivers. But now roads very good. Now just four and a half hours in a minivan to make 107 miles. Much better now. Shorter."

℘   But the trip was long enough for it all to come back once more, those pictures of a place and a people caught in a war. They are hiding in mosquito-breeding marshes and rice fields, peeking out from behind bushes, perched on platforms that prop up shacks on stilts, splashing through muddy streams and puddles whose sultriness rises from them—visibly—even in the darkness of night. Big burly figures bearing guns in those silty rivers, lifting high their ammo as they sink from ankle to knee to waist to chest to elbow. Stalking. Breast-feeding mothers washing their other children and the week's laundry—or is it the month's?—in those puddles and brown rivers, smiling nervously as the white one passes by. Even now, they look toward me with what seems a mix of worry and wonder, terror and expectation: Friend or foe?

℘   In the heart of the Mekong Delta, Cantho, Vietnam's deep south, the land of Nine Dragons that

symbolize nine rivers, we must notify the government authorities that a white man from the United
States is staying in a private home, "the nice home."
The house is beautiful—*dep lam.* It is modest,
sparkling clean, with electricity and limited water
pressure for shower and toilet, all refurbished with
the help of the monies sent by the *Viet Kieu:* Bao and
his family. This house butts up against, or rather
props up the shanty next door with earthen floor
and colorless walls, where the family—mother, father,
cousins, aunts, uncles, more aunts and uncles—hud-
dles together while Bao and I sleep on bamboo mats
in the new house. The shanty is where, after the fall
of Saigon, little Bao and his brothers and sisters
played in summertime while their mother went to
work each day, and their father remained imprisoned in the reeducation camp in the north.

    ☞   It is here that we will celebrate *Tet:* in a
house, amidst a family, the way it is supposed to be.
It is Bao's first celebration of *Tet* in Cantho since he
and his family fled the country. And for the others,
it is the first celebration of *Tet* with a white man, the

first ever to kick off his shoes and cross the threshold into their home.

The dishes of regional foods are ready for our tasting, the altar table set for the veneration of ancestors. *Ao dai* are cleaned and pressed to perfection, anticipating midnight fireworks that will ring in the first day of the Year of the Monkey. The magnificent yellow *mai,* brought fresh from the flower market, lights up the new house with its own kind of shimmering electricity. We head off for the pre-*Tet* celebrations on puttering cruise ships along the Mekong. There we watch magicians and thump to the music of the dancing dragon, sipping freshly crushed fruit drinks and Tiger Beer, tasting the nightlife of Cantho. In the morning, we visit the floating market on one river of the Nine Dragons, where boats' lips kiss as flowers are exchanged for fish, or eel is traded for dried spices without anyone ever setting foot on land.

☙   Chanh forgoes joining us in these festivities. He is finishing his house chores or working at the new computer. Hardly serious, he displays his fascination with the computer alongside a playful, good-humored hospitality toward the visitors—one quite strange—who have come for *Tết* festival. He is ready to give me quick lessons in Vietnamese. I, in turn, instruct him in English. He is better than he thinks. Like his cousin Bao, he likes the idioms, words like "e-mail chatting."

Wrapped in a capellini-thin body with strong hands that reach near-knee length when standing poker straight, the twenty-something Chanh demonstrates the maturity of a man twice his age. He is the consummately dutiful son, loyal to the ancestors, faithful to family, and, above all, heir to the family name, carrier of the family line, the only one of this whole lot of cousins to be both eldest and male. The only first son in a world in which family and ancestry, the lines and links formed by blood, give shape to who and what this family is and everything they might ever become.

☞   The photos of the ancestors hang in the home's finest room, caressed by wisps of fragrant incense, their memories honored by rhythmic bowing and by the altars laden with their favorite foods, including a cold Tiger Beer for Bao's maternal grandfather. I need to remind myself over and over that they practice ancestor veneration. They are not Christian, save one. And the one who is Christian is one of them before anything else.

Designations such as Christian or Catholic or, from my youth, "pagan" or "heathen" slip off them. It is not their faith, under whatever name, that binds me to them in this house of belonging. It is what I can only name as their un-say-able way of *life-ing*—the sheer aliveness that pulsates in their hearts. They live each day close to the earth, seemingly on the edge of living and dying every moment of each day. A people who have lost so much, yet still have room enough at hearth and table for me and reserves aplenty in the ways of the heart for one who unknowingly has come all this way to learn its ways.

☞ We gather in the evening before the altar of veneration. Husbands and wives bow—quick and dutiful—in unison in the presence of the ancestors. They are followed in turns by the young adults, the teens, the little girls in their high heels and ribboned hair. Bao and Thay Tam are saluted by the eldest of the aunts. They thank us profusely for honoring the family: Bao for returning to the family to celebrate *Tet* and to honor their ancestors; me for all that I have taught Bao and for the help given him in fulfilling his dreams. Such a short rite: Home, family, elders; word and gesture; memory, thanks, and hope. What more is there?

We then pour out into the streets together with all the others in Cantho, as the heart of the Nine Dragons beats with all the anticipation of the moment, of a lifetime, of a people, waiting for the sky brightened and ablaze in fireworks, as echoes of *Chuc Mung Nam Moi! Happy New Year!* ring throughout the neighborhood.

Chuc Mung Nam Moi: one of the few phrases I learned in those days. The New Year is the occasion not only for honoring and for welcoming the ancestors into the family home, but it is the moment to offer luck, prosperity, and longevity to all the living. *Tet* greetings are always accompanied by best wishes for a long and healthy life and success in all undertakings. A sign of luck is the custom of giving *li xi*, lucky money, tucked in those little red and gold envelops I had seen years ago on the trees brought into chapel and dining room at the seminary in

Camarillo. In Cantho and elsewhere children run randomly through the streets with hands outstretched hoping for *li xi* from any and all who pass by.

     ℘   Back at the house, one by one, each family member lines up and comes in turn to wish me *Chuc Mung Nam Moi,* extending to me their hope for all the luck, prosperity, and longevity a life could hold—first the little girls, then the teens, then the young women and men, finally the adults. Each one offers their good wishes and receives the *li xi* that I place in their palms, the gratitude showing in that gentle bow.

The line's end appears in sight with the dawning realization that Chanh is not here. A collective annoyance gives way to a sigh of relief as he then appears. Racing breathlessly to the entrance of the house, kicking off his flip-flops at entry, hair mussed, dragging black pant legs sweeping the cool cement floor, rose-colored shirt tales flapping like breeze-blown sails—he lunges up the stairs three at a time. Balancing the two still-burning incense sticks from the nearby temple where he had been to ring in *Tet,* he bears now in his body the blessing of temple to home and family. He is breathless in the first hour of this New Year. All the duty, all the reverence, all the delight of this night-giving-way-to-day is carried in the heart of the boy who has brought the blessing.

Last in line, he comes shyly, peeking over the shoulders of those ahead of him in the line of well-wishers. There is the gentle bow, two hands extended with such grace, gnarled knuckles and calloused palms rendering beauty's balm. The nervous grin I know. It is...Thuan's! Am I there or here; here or there? Cantho or Camarillo? I am new to this place, a stranger made welcome in a place which is not a place at all, but an ever-widening circle, cycle of belonging.

☞   Chanh: you stand before me bearing the weight of a world, the hope of a family, of those gone before and those still to come, on shoulders bigger and broader than your frame can seem to bear. Yet you bear the hope and promise, the fear and anxiety, all the darkness and light one heart can hold. You quiver, eyes flickering with the light of every star that has ever kissed you with promise. It is a whole world—and every desire of the human heart is in that glance, that single instant that bridges worlds, melts years, ties tongues. Every region of it, all its geography, the longitudes and latitudes of the human heart are charted in the contours of one face, in the opening of this single smile, in the moist and mist of those eyes. I see a million wordless wonders in a glance:

Unspeakable,
the language of a face.
One face, a world.

Every word spoken; to be spoken
said in the saying of your face.

Each moment, every movement of a life
ticking timelessly in the traces of that face.

One face.
Seeing. Gazing. Behold(ing).

In one look, you see me, the all of me.

Corners, cracks of a life now steeped, now
    soaked and saturated
by each motionless movement of a face that
    knows how to see,
loving beyond the reach of wor(l)ds.

Endless words in one beat of a heart:

Come

    Stay

        Away

Seeing by loving; loving by seeing

    a whole world

in the light streaming out of the two eyes of

    you.

The hope of a world

in your smile.

☞ "Uh oh! Time to go. Move on." So Bao greets the morning of our departure from Cantho. For days his voice had been ringing through the paper thin walls of his maternal family home, gleeful notes of Vietnamese melodies, blissful cooing, sounds from him and his cousins as they relive childhood memories. But this day a quiet has come over him. It's the first day of the Year of the Monkey. And Bao has already cried his goodbyes quietly, alone. It appears that, in Vietnam, this is how it's done: parting with handshakes rather than embraces; the stiff upper lip rather than the wringing of tear-drenched handkerchiefs.

In Saigon once more, the days following brought me ever more deeply into the widening circle of these small, bone-thin people who love to eat; the ones who cry alone. In the last days, there were the hours of searching for the best bowl of *pho,* slurping one last *ca phe sua da,* that luscious coffee with sweet milk over ice, loading up with souvenirs, certain as I could be that this would be my one and only visit to Vietnam, to these people and this land.

The day before we departed Vietnam, Chanh, his sister Loan, and cousin Thang made the hours-long journey back from Cantho to Saigon to bid us farewell. Bao reminded them to bring money so that they could buy something to eat on the way, but there was no money. When they arrived, we fed them from whatever we had at hand.

℞   There was packing to do. Every item to be weighed on an old fruit scale carried all the way from the land of the Nine Dragons to Saigon. Each of the two boxes allotted to Bao and to me had no more than seventy pounds. And not one ounce less. We crammed the four boxes with dried fish and Hue candies, dark coffee and computer books in Vietnamese, *ao dai* and handicrafts from Sapa, Hanoi, and Saigon.

Through the night we packed. In the hours before dawn, everyone stretched out on bamboo mats, dozens of them in two small rooms. Short one bamboo mat, Thang and Chanh had to sleep side by side on sheets spread out on the floor. All slept easily, save one. The sadness of our leaving gripped me now as I heard those outside my window gathering in the church at 4:00 A.M. As I lay awake on this last night, the voices in the church were once more raised in thanks to God. And this night, as on the first, my poor prayer found its voice in the language of weeping. I joined them, all of them, in giving thanks to God, and to Our Lady of La Vang, for bringing us here, for all that I had been given by this people and by this land.

✺   En route to the Saigon airport, it was I who silently wept, already anticipating the ache of absence...a quiet lament in the back seat of a taxi. I dared not make much of our leaving, for the pain was more theirs than mine. Cousin Thang offered more comfort than he'll ever know: "Thay Tam, you will never leave Vietnam. Your heart stays with us here."

On arriving, we found them there already. All those who had come to greet us were there now to send us on our way. And there were more still, those many who had welcomed us along the way. Carried by a wave of *bon voyage* from taxi to airport entrance, it was as though I had fallen deep into some sea of dreams. I heard it again: that ringing, those chimes, that delighted and delighting chirping chatter: "Take a picture!" And as if in a moment, we were gone from them. So quick, of a sudden. How unlike the long and mournful partings of my race—the Irish. There were no tears among these people, just "Time to go. Move on."

☞   Now past the check-in counter, I turned to look once more—Irishman that I am—at those arms stretching in the air, hands waving, bodies hopping from one foot to another to see, a dozen smiles in that sea of open arms that had welcomed me just eighteen days before. I kept straining for one last look, for one picture that would last me a lifetime, the face that I could look to in place of all the dusty pictures lodged for so long in the dusty corners of my heart's memory of Vietnam.

As I realized in the next few moments, that face had been before me all the while. Gazing from the window at takeoff, counting the seconds on his digital watch as we raced down the runway, Bao turned and looked at me. He whispered: "Homeland." There was then that space of quiet when travelers seem to look back in silence over all the days and miles shared. It was he who broke the silence: "Almost lunchtime!" And then he asked me, as he always has done: "How do we say it?" And we chanted together: "A nation of small, bronzed, bone-thin people...who love to eat!" Two or three times, singsong. As he chuckles, I hear the echoes of a happy child singing in that house in Cantho. "Better still," I said, adding a little emphasis for fun, "a nation of small, bronzed, bone-thin people *consumed* with eating."

Unexpectedly, he blankly stares. A tear. And then another, then more and more. The first time I have ever seen him cry. Quiet, huge tears rolling down both sides of his face. Crying. Weeping. But not alone: Faithful Teacher took the hand of Faithful Student to offer some small comfort.

Bao quivered and then gulped deep: "I know why."

"We were always so hungry. My father. In that camp. Up there. That place. We went there. Lao Cai, close to China. My mother went to work so she could bring home money to buy lunch. Every day we waited and waited. Alone, in that house where we went for *Tet,* in Cantho. There was nothing to eat. So hungry. All the time. *This* is why we love to eat. I *am* that hungry boy."

At that moment, through those tears, Bao smiled—and I had the picture of the face I would take with me for always. It was the face of that hungry, crying boy with me all along. In that one glance I found yet again the face of hope, the hope that I had come to know in Thuan's graceful bowing to death, and in Chanh's bearing the blessing to his home and family and people, carrying them forward with all the hope one heart can hold.

☙　The Word of Love created the world. Now another word—Tam, Heart—created a new world for me. "Thay Tam. They want to call you Thay Tam." They named me "Heart," and called me to life once more, helping me to fall in love as if for the first time with them and with their place, their land, the home-land. It was not so much their faith that called, but the *life-ing* of a people made sinewy strong in affliction. It is so much: the sensuality, the pulsating utter aliveness, the surpassing dignity of carriage, the exquisite grace of their bearing, and the majestic contours of that terrain—so lush and deep and green and blue and purple—that they opened to me, showed me. A numbed, tired, and tarred heart has been taught to see and to love anew.

From where this lesson? From somewhere—the spare rooms of Cantho, the Shrine at La Vang, the early morning Mass at Saigon, perhaps the torch-song crooning midnight divas—I cannot remember. And whether their language or mine—I am uncer-tain. What does it matter? The words are clear. My ears have never heard these words, but I now know the language, as it beats into eternity from one awak-ened heart: far beyond every endless sky, deeper than any dark sea, a love that knows no end stirs my heart again. The unlocking of a heart. *This* heart. A heart that learned that it is never too late to learn how to look, how to see.

❧ "Take a picture!" In it they are all there—Phaolo, Kiet, Miss Huong, Sau, Cha John Baptist, and Cha Lam, the aunts and uncles, little cousins in glittering high heels. The face of each one fixed to a canvas the length and width and breadth and depth of one weary heart stretched mightily to open and receive their welcome.

I, too, am there. In the picture. At the heart of the Nine Dragons, ringing in the Year of the Monkey, I am seeing, I am gazing, I am beholding the hope of a whole world in one smile. And in the tear-soaked face of a hungry boy ripped from his homeland, my heart has found the bridge from here to there, from there to here.

Part Two

Image Reflections
on Life in the Spirit

On Learning How to Look

Contemplation and Transparency

❧   Saint Paul has it that faith comes by hearing. Words matter. What we say counts. What we hear forms us from the very first moment of our lives, for good or for ill. But even more, we are shaped by what we see. Images, pictures, religious and computer icons sink into our psyche.

Few are likely to remember the precise words used to announce the events of September 11, 2001. But who can forget the image of the World Trade Center's Twin Towers crumbling to the ground after being pierced by the United and American Airlines jets hijacked by suicidal terrorists?

How will we live with the images, now etched in the eye of a nation, of U.S. military men and women abusing those entrusted to their care in the prisons of Iraq? No doubt each of those who humiliated the Iraqi prisoners began their military service with noble intentions. The images serve as a reminder of how easily our own good intentions can go astray.

In the same way, what words of John Paul II will be remembered through history is yet to be known. But the image of the young and vigorous traveling missionary Pope is lodged in our mind's eye, along-side that of the frail and faltering pontiff of the new millennium. Looking to him, some wonder if the diminished Holy Father is able to lead the Church of which he is head. Others, like Jean Vanier—founder of the world-wide l'Arche communities, wherein mentally handicapped and the so-called "normal" live together of the spirit of the Beatitudes—comment that he has never been more beautiful, seeing in his weakness and vulnerability the presence of the self-emptying of Christ about which he has written so eloquently.

✎ We think from what we see, we picture ideas, we dream in living color or in black and white. Pictures elicit our feelings in ways that words sometimes do not. Image shapes our understanding of God, of Christ, of the Spirit. Statues of saints and icons of Mary, of angels, of martyrs from throughout Christian history and our own day fill out the Catholic imagination. We picture Christ as Good Shepherd, Sacred Heart, Suffering Servant, Teacher, Preacher, Healer, or Companion on the journey. These images of Christ are important to the life of faith, as is what we hear from him or of him. Faith comes from hearing. But it is cultivated, nurtured, and sustained by what is seen.

Awash in the sea of images all around us—on billboards, television, computer screens, in magazines, newspapers—it is easy to become numb to their influence upon us. But images last, they stick, they are not easily dislodged. In a consumerist culture such as ours, in which images are used to appeal to our appetites—"Drink me! Buy me! Smoke me! Eat me! Wear me!" and, most of all, "Look like me and *be* like me!"—we learn how to discriminate. We must sift chaff from wheat, cheap fare from what is good and noble to strengthen the spirit. The image of the good life—luxury cruises, never-ending leisure time, money to burn, an eternally youthful body mingled with that of another—is not how Christians pledge to make good on the one and only life they have to live.

🖎 The good life for the Christian is seen and heard in the image of the Reign of God. Jesus proclaimed the Reign of God as the fulfillment of God's hope, desire, and intention for the world now and to come. In God's Reign, truth, holiness, justice, love, and peace will hold sway forever. Such is the *true* or *real* good life. And the cost of *this* good life is seen in the Crucified One who gives himself as a gift so that others might have life and have it to the full. Behold! Light, Life, and Love—the Love of God given to the world—crucified and stretched out on a tree, pouring forth life to the world even and especially in his dying, death, and descent into hell.

Sifting through what is deserving of our seeing, being discriminating in what we will give our eyes to, discerning what is worthy of our looking, means that we must train and discipline the eye. Whatever may be said of seeing with the eye of the heart, it is first a matter of actually paying attention, focusing the eye, looking at and into something without distraction. Our gift and task is to learn how to see anew each day, learning how to look. Christian faith is a whole way of life, a way of seeing by loving. The more we see, the more we love. The more we love, the more we see. Refining, purifying our eye allows us to see each and every one, everything and every living creature, deeply. To read the world and all that is in it with love.

℘   This is how the contemplative sees. Not all are called to the contemplative life in the strict and formal sense of those who give their lives to steady, disciplined, routine prayer, often within an enclosed monastic environment. But all who are baptized into Christ in the gift of the Spirit may be awakened to the contemplative dimension of everyday living. How so?

Central to the contemplative life is the discipline of *lectio divina,* sacred reading. The contemplative reads often and deeply, primarily from the Scriptures. The eyes fall to the text and are kissed by pulsating images of a God who is Shepherd and Companion, Vanguard and Shield, crucified Mercy for the life of the world. But as this abundance of images take hold of the mind and heart of the contemplative, the eyes learn how to read and to see the presence of God in all of human life, in the events of the here and now, in the life of the Church, and in the wide, wonderful, and often whacked-out world.

Learning how to read all life long is the gift and task of the contemplative. To be awakened to the contemplative dimension of everyday living means that the eye must be like that of an eagle, sharp and surveying, penetrating and focused. It is not so much about saying one's prayers at all the appointed times and places. It is, rather, more about praying all the time—praying by looking. By seeing. By reading as a whole way of life.

The contemplative is all eyes. But these eyes are the eyes of the heart. The contemplative sees everything—with love. Love, the life that pours itself forth in self-giving. The more we love with love's look, the more we see. And the more we see, the more we love.

❧ As I write, I am beginning the annual retreat for sixty-five Benedictine monks at Conception Abbey in Missouri. The conferences take place in the monastery adjacent to the newly renovated church—a stunning jewel chiseled in the manner of the ornate style of the monastery of Beuron in the Black Forest of Germany. But the renovation has made the church of Conception Abbey open and airy. Its wide and clean open spaces allow natural light to caress the church's interior. The eye is lifted to the glistening frescoes on the ceiling—rusts and golds, deep purples and ivory adorning the figures and faces of Saint Benedict and Saint Scholastica, the near-stoic serenity of biblical men and women, gilded-wings on the angels crowning Mary Queen. Over the entrance of the church there is a splendid circular stained-glass window. There, in brilliant blue and silvery-white, we see Christ the High Priest flanked by two angels, messengers of God's peace and good will. They join with the one who lays down his life in self-giving love to the Father, offering himself for the life of the world.

The sound of the monks in choir is some of the finest chant I have heard in English. At Vespers this early summer evening, as the psalmody lilts heavenward, the sun's bright orange-red ball is setting, casting a warm glow through that window—heaven's light embracing and bathing the whole of the church in and through the love of Christ given for us.

℞ Monks, anticipating the suppression of their monastery by hostile political forces, fled Switzerland and founded Conception Abbey in 1873. They planted themselves deep in the undulating hillocks of northwestern Missouri. No one simply "stops by" Conception Abbey; you have to go out of your way to get to this remote farmland nearing the Kansas, Iowa, and Nebraska borders. Thus, on June 10, 2002, one man traveled ninety miles to get there.

With a shotgun and plenty of ammunition in his car, he drove into the parking lot at Conception. He entered the church that morning, passing under the window of Christ's self-offering. He worked his way quietly into the monastery and then shot four monks—killing two and wounding another two. There was no apparent reason. He had no association with the monks. They did not know him or know of him. As the monks scrambled to make sense of what was happening in their midst, the gunman went to the church and took his own life by a bullet to his head.

On my arrival to begin the retreat, Abbot Gregory told me the story of the four monks: the names of those whose lives had been taken from them; how the lives of the others had been altered forever because of that event. I listened. But it did not all sink in until he brought me to the place where Philip had been shot and died. The bullet hole remains in the wooden floor near the monastery parlor. I looked. And I bent low to touch. And I prayed. All of Gregory's narrative, told in hushed and still-mournful tones, did not touch me in the same way as seeing the mark of the bullet in the floor, the place where an elderly monk lay bleeding from the head and dying. I have already forgotten most of Gregory's carefully detailed narrative, but I shall live with the image of that pierced floor.

℘ I wander through that church looking at the high ceilings and frescoes, the sight of rose windows and altar, ambo and font. All visually near perfect. The rattling of rosary beads echo from one of the back pews. A novice in blue jeans and T-shirt sweeping the monks' stalls in the choir. These sounds of hushed, quiet movements soothe because of the braided inlaid brickwork of the floor. Leaving the church, I saunter through the monastic corridor and look at the photos of two monks, discretely hung

over the place where each died, the bullet of senseless violence taking both of them within minutes on
an early June morning. Snatched from this haven of
peace without warning. I bend low again to see that
hole, that scar, that wound in a wooden floor. To
gaze upon it and to touch. Touching that wound, I
whisper a prayer for the monk I never knew but
whose life has marked mine forever through the
image of a bullet that ripped through his head and
scarred the wooden floor on which his brothers continue to trod in their life of daily work and prayer.

℞   But of them all, the image that remains is
this: a picture, a photograph, taken by a journalist
who had arrived on the scene of the crime that day.
There are two officers of the peace, one the local
sheriff, each with a pistol on his hip. They are hur-
rying the monks—some quite aged and infirm—from
the monastery, searching furiously to discover if the
gunman was lone. Are there others on the grounds?
In the monastery? The church? The library? The
panic pours from their faces all over this picture.

Walking with them, his pectoral cross dangling
over his black robe as his long scapular flaps in the

breeze, is Gregory, the spiritual father of the community. The Abbot. There is boldness in his face. There is, too, a shade of sorrow that softens the defiance in those eyes, his Czech chin protruding slightly forward as he marches on alongside the two officers. That one face—that indelible image—says it all, in a way that words could never tell: "We will not be ruled by fear."

Love's Gaze

Reverence and Discernment

🕊 She is an art collector. The art of the South Pacific is her specialty. She has an eye for it. She can pick out the real thing from the junk. Her fortune has been built on a discerning eye; knowing how to focus on what is good and set aside the rest. In an instant, she can tell what is true and what is false, an original from an imitation. Pouring over some recent photographs, she pulled one toward her for a closer look. "I'll bet he's smart," was her comment as she peered at the photo. She was not referring to baby Em being held in my arms, but to the student, naturally photogenic, who leaned in next to us. "Yes, he is," I agreed. "Quite bright." With a twinkle she added, "You can see the brains in some people's eyes."

How true! You can see the intelligence in people's eyes. And you can see so much more: the dullness, the darkness, the elation, the envy, the care and crassness, the boldness and the bashfulness, the anger and the ache of absence. A whole world, a story told and awaiting telling, the lines of a life are all there. Age-old wisdom has it that the eyes are the windows to the soul. But eyes tell their story when they are gazed into...we must look each other in the face.

🖙 The Jewish philosopher, Emmanuel Levinas, paid particular attention to the human face. A survivor of the Holocaust, who died in Paris in 1995, he had seen and suffered because of humanity's inhumanity to humanity: six million Jews and six million others lost their lives through human brutality and barbarism at the hands of a people whose homeland was deeply religious, and Christian. For Levinas, this was proof that both religious and secular ideals no longer seemed capable of providing people with a clear sense of right and wrong. He set out to find new guidelines, probing the mystery of good and evil, looking for the foundation of the moral life, for a basis on which to anchor the good life. Finally, shaped through and through by his experience of excruciating human suffering, Levinas's search for a new moral touchstone brought his gaze to rest upon the human face.

☞   A call to goodness, a moral claim, is made upon me in the face of "the other," a flesh-and-blood human being, a person. When the other looks at me, wanting, needing—be it food, or shelter, or clothing, or love, or understanding, or freedom—something is called forth from me. In the gaze of the other—those eyes bespeaking need, desperation, depression, anguish, and hope—there is an invitation to do some good. To love, to understand, to let the other be free. But even more, to let the other *live,* to do what is needed to cultivate, nurture, and sustain the life of the other, this one who is so different from me and who invites me into another world, a world of difference, a whole new world of longing, of desire, of need. And in so doing, inviting me to do some small good.

This may be all we can manage in our day and age. So many today live with an uneasy sense that there is no longer a "big picture." For many people— deeply religious people no less—the world doesn't hang together the way we once thought it did. This puts a bold question mark before our understanding of God and how God relates to the world. God the all-powerful monarch, arranging and controlling the universe, seems simply beyond belief. And when this understanding of God flies in the face of experience, the worldview that rests upon it also begins to crumble. Attempting to agree on certain non-negotiable elements of a coherent worldview seems futile. Consequently, there are no commonly held values that provide a sense of shared purpose. Why be good? Why tell the truth? Why do the right thing? On what basis?

Instead of beginning with worldviews, we can begin small. With the face of the other. So much evil might be avoided when the gaze of the other penetrates my soul, my conscience, with those eyes that plead: "Don't kill me. Please let me live." Looking deeply into the gazing eyes of the other, seeing there the contours of every human story, even and especially my own, I find the foundation for the possibility of doing good, of living a good life.

☙ We were talking over his life. It was a "life-inventory" of sorts, a retrospective of days well-lived at a rather late hour in his life. I pointed to his many awards, his various teaching assignments, his widely-acclaimed essays and books. Then there were the administrative posts, the offices held in learned societies, the joys of wife and family. We moved on to the way perspective is easily lost in the face of the many pressing demands of life in our day and age. We offered words of support to one another amidst struggles to be faithful to a Church that promises the grace of ongoing conversion for greater authenticity in Gospel-living, but increasingly seems to reign people in and make it more difficult for them to live with integrity, in holiness, truth, justice, love, and peace.

He leaned back, sipping an after-dinner drink: "In view of all the achievements and the setbacks, I reckon that all that really matters is what happens person to person." The distinguished professor's parting comment to me that evening: "Person to person; face to face." But I can only truly see "person to person" if I look with respect.

🖎　Ten years after our graduation, my college classmate sat near me on the couch in his now-empty living room. His perfect marriage was now in a shambles. I listened to him recount the various events that had led to their parting, the divorce of the proverbial dream couple atop a wedding cake. After a while, knowing we were circling the issue, I finally asked him bluntly: "What's the real story? What really happened?" He responded quietly, carefully, candidly, "We lost respect for each other. You remember, from the Latin roots, *re-spect* means to look again, to look once more. We stopped looking at one another again and again with eyes that really know how to see. When we lost respect for each other, our marriage began to die."

Christians learn early on that they should try to *see* Christ in the other, in the neighbor, even in the enemy. In my early years in a closely-knit (and sometimes tightly-closed!) Irish Catholic community in southwest Philadelphia, I gazed upon the face of Jesus: the Good Shepherd in our hallway, the Heavenly Jesus pointing to his Sacred Heart enthroned in our living room, and the little Infant Jesus in the Christmas manger. And I tried with all my might to see *this* Jesus in my neighbor.

In later years, no doubt due to my melancholic Irish temperament, I found annoying, if not outright offensive, those watercolors made popular in the 1970s and 1980s in which Jesus is a sort of thirty-something howling holy hyena lifting babies in the style of a politician on the campaign trail, or surrounded by teenagers as if practicing camp songs with the local Boy Scouts. Granted, there was a much-needed corrective to the preponderance of grim-faced eyes turned to heaven while praying in a purple-shadowed Gethsemane. Yet, while the "Smiling Jesus" images invited me to see a very human Jesus as my best pal, it was also hard to see *this* Jesus in most of my neighbors.

When instructed to "see Christ in the other," we often take one of these familiar images to plaster *onto* the face of neighbor or enemy. We read Christ *into* the other, rather than allowing the other to manifest something of the mystery of Christ by being who they are. How does the other, in all her otherness and difference, allow Christ to "stand forth," to shine in and through him precisely *as* another?

Pondering this question, living with, holding, cradling these things in the heart as Mary did, something gestates into life in and through us, as it did in and through her. It may take more time than we would like, but gradually we do understand. We glimpse the truth of the other, at times in the blink of an eye: "I see."

℘ At the Los Angeles Religious Congress, a grand and glorious gathering of people from every race, land, and language, I stood together with nearly 20,000 others for the concluding Sunday Liturgy. I found myself once again pondering what seemed to be something of a conundrum: Seeing Christ in the other. *Which* Christ? *How* and *where* do I see Christ?

As often happens in the context of prayer and worship, I slip off—or am carried—into a moment outside time, a place which is no *place* at all. Amid the sounds and the movements and the sights and smells of these 20,000 people, I now see faces of the human family—Mexican, Vietnamese, Filipino, Nigerian, Euro-White, men and women, mothers with babies, grandmothers and teenage boys, prom queens in the making in their low-rise jeans—a wide and deep sea of humanity by which I am buoyed up. It is in that moment that I have some sense of who Christ might be, not by seeing him in the other, but by receiving in the glance of each of these others some trace of a Face whose contours I must squint to discern...for the light is blinding. I do not see Christ in them. Rather, Christ is looking at me in and through each of them, all of them, those who are— member for member—the Body, whose eyes now peer at me in and through them all. Person-to-person to person-to-person, I have some vague sense of see-ing who Christ might be.

In the deeper movements of prayer there are no words. There is only the embrace of silence that takes us and carries us toward Unspeakable Mystery. Wrapped in the Word beneath and beyond all words, we see, not all at once, but slowly, shielding our eyes to gain some small glimpse. We want to see, but the light is blinding. We search and strain to see the Face. We want to see, to look upon the face of God.

In our searching and seeking, we sometimes scramble and fret. We get anxious in prayer. Or bored and distracted. Or disappointed and discouraged. We are ready to give up. It is then and there that the gift is being offered: be still. Rest. Receive the gaze of the Other. It is not so much that we must turn to God to seek that Face. It is, rather, more that the Face of the Other is turned toward us. But we, restless and anxious and fretting, allow the mind and heart to fill with the overlay of words and images that we say and see *into* God. And yet, despite this, that Face seeks us. Searches us out. The Face of that Other who makes a claim on my life: wanting me, all of me, every inch and ounce of me...and us all.

🐦 In searching for us, God sees *through* loving, *in* loving, *with* loving—eyes near-mauve with mercy, penetrating in their long and loving gaze upon us. "You can see the *brains* in those eyes." And so much more: every face, every movement of the human heart, every event of the human story—all its agony and pain, the struggle for freedom and life—all shining through the eyes of that Face, the Face gazing upon me here and now, at this time and in this place. The eyes say it all: "Let me live. Please let me live. In you. Through you. With you. Person to person. Face to face."

The Boldness of Bowing

Humility and Solidarity

❧   A real Plain Jane. No makeup on her face. No jewelry or perfume. A somber muted-patterned dress well past her knees when miniskirts were all the rage. Black penny loafers without old Indian-head pennies to adorn them. Her thinning hair was very closely cropped, a page-boy cut, like a young Mia Farrow. I wondered if she had lost her hair from the heavy starched linen and veil she had worn in the convent all that time. In the years following the Second Vatican Council, her religious superiors sent her for studies. A few other sisters took studies in music or theology; in her case, it was philosophy— and she was very bright. In the course of her doctoral studies, she decided to follow another path. She was now professor of philosophy at Villanova University, and my teacher.

I didn't notice it in the classroom; there were too many of us. But I noticed it when I saw her interacting with others. A sort of tilting or nodding of the head. Later she told us that she had the practice of nodding her head whenever she encountered another person. This was her gesture of respect for the other person, a slight bow, a sign of attention to the Holy Spirit dwelling within them. She reminded us that everyone was a temple of the Holy Spirit, even non-Catholics, which was for me back then a rather daring idea! In my fancy I imagined her on one of those jam-packed trains from Villanova to the heart of center city Philadelphia, her head bobbing in a sea of commuters. Steadying herself by holding on tight as the train lunged forward and screeched to a halt, the anonymous former nun bowing unbeknownst to all these temples of the Holy Spirit.

✍ In our own time and place bowing seems an antiquated practice of the royal court; a simple handshake will do, thank you very much! We do not have royalty, and yet most have seen films in which a messenger or explorer or soldier bows before the king or queen, a flourish of deference to His Lordship or Her Ladyship. Often regarded as a sign of sub-servience, the gesture of someone lesser in the presence of a greater figure, bowing is a custom that never held a prominent place in our culture.

In the main, we do not think to bow even in church—except for monastics, who keep the practice alive, bowing profoundly from the waist at the conclusion of each psalm said or sung in choir. Monks and nuns, men and women, also bow down before the altar in coming and going from the church. They bow before a crucifix in the dining room. In some places they bow before the Abbot or Abbess. When they pronounce their monastic vows, they bow so deeply that they lie prostrate on the floor, close to the earth. Instead, most of us Catholics genuflect; a quick down and up if we can manage it.

☙   Cultures that embrace bowing tangibly express the truth that the "other" is a unique other: particular, irreplaceable, someone who, no matter how close, is a mystery. Without this sense of the mystery of the other, of the necessary distance between us, of the sheer veil of otherness that will always remain between us, we sink and suffocate in a swamp of false closeness to others. The illusion? All of us as everyone's buddy in one big happy family! In a world of first names, where the surname— one's sense of origin and belonging by blood—seems incidental, our sense of depersonalization, estrangement, and alienation has never been more pronounced. In an "in your face" culture, we need a little more distance, that necessary ingredient of intimacy. We need to take time to stand back, exercise a little reserve (dare I say good manners?), and learn how to bow gently, gracefully, softly as a sign of respect, indeed reverence, for the other person.

℘ We may have seen comedy films which show Asian people, often Japanese, one bowing before the other, who in turn bows and is greeted by the other's bow in what looks like a kind of contest to determine who can outdo the other. But I speak here of the more gracious and gentle bow of Asian cultures, soft and low, often with hands folded and fingers pointed upward in respect.

☞   When traveling to South Korea with a former Korean-American student who was all-but-fully
Westernized, he stated prior to our arrival in Seoul,
"The first thing I must do when we get there, before
anything else, is go to my father's mother's house
and pay my respect to her." Thinking that this was a
simple courtesy call, I remarked, "Can we go there
later in the day, after we shake this jet lag?" The
answer was gentle yet firm, "No, I must go there first,
to make my bows before her, to show my respect for
the elders, for the ancestors, for the family."

☞   When we bow, we lower ourselves. We bend
toward the other and incline our bodies toward the
ground, the earth. We may not see eye to eye, but we
may look to the feet of the other and see them planted firmly on the earth. Whatever their stance, they
are part of this earth. From it they have come and to
it they will return. As will I. Bowing, however slightly or profoundly before another, serves to remind us
that we are all part of created reality, and that this
creation has been embraced in the Incarnation—the
becoming flesh, becoming earthen—of God, by bending down, by bowing toward us.

This bending low of God is the divine condescension. And, as might be expected, it finds a more prominent place in Eastern than Western Christian traditions. The term does not suggest that God is condescending or demeaning. It is rather that God bows down to the earth and pours out divine love among the lowly of the earth. One scriptural image that helps us understand this bowing of God toward us is *kenosis* or self-emptying.

Kenosis is nothing more, or less, than the mystery of God's identification with the human reality. But *kenosis* has a particular slant, informed by a singular insight. And the insight is that of self-emptying, best understood in light of Saint Paul's letter to the Philippians, chapter 2, Second Corinthians 12:8–10, as well as First Corinthians 1:18 and following, wherein human wisdom is contrasted with the folly of the cross.

❧ From the vantage point of *kenosis,* God comes to earth and earthly reality without pretense, in contrast to human arrogance. The *kenosis* puts a question mark in front of the ways we relate to ourselves, the other, others, God, and, indeed, every living creature. The divine mystery does not rest in the loftiness, the grandeur, or otherworldliness of God, but rather in the fact that God should appear in such a fashion.

Kenosis is the scene on which God appears, refusing to identify with human loftiness and self-importance. Such hauteur defies the logic of the gift of self-emptying love, the pouring forth of divine life in order to appear on the scene of human weakness and vulnerability, in order to identify with human beings in the concrete circumstances of their lives. This is a God who is present amid human longing and want. This is the meaning of God's *kenosis:* bending low enough to embrace human flesh and the events of human life and history—bending so low as to wash the feet that trod dusty, sometimes filthy, paths of the earth.

The *kenosis* calls us to a way of discipleship in which we are to stand beneath the cross, at the feet of the crucified Christ. It requires resistance to any claim to a power that controls, manipulates, dominates. Its only power is the ability to effect change through service. And as those who serve, as Christ did through divine condescension, we cannot be above bowing low before the other, no matter how lowly they may be or what our standing in life.

The bow expresses a commitment to solidarity with all those who have been pushed and shoved down, those who are often voiceless, useless, a nuisance—the lowly of the earth, those at the bottom of the various rankings in the Church—recognizing that it is *precisely there* that the heart of the Church is to be found. Living faith at the bottom, even and especially of the Church, we learn how to bow not simply as a churchy, religious gesture, but as a permanent factor of our existence, to bow before the one whose generous descent made of God one of the lowly of the earth; bowing too before those last, littlest, and least among us who are promised to be first in rank in the Reign of God.

One of these "least" is the woman "bent-double" with an unnamed crippling, debilitating disease. In the Gospel according to Luke (13:10–17) we can see her approaching Jesus to beg for healing. And he who bent toward us in his self-emptying in the crib and on the cross does heal her, no doubt bending yet again to reach a woman hunched over, whose eyes strain upward to catch a glimpse of those hands stretched out to be placed upon her.

☙   Taken down from the cross, the body of Jesus was laid in a tomb, put down into the earth. One of the central mysteries of the Christian faith is so often neglected in our preaching, teaching, and celebration of Christ's mysteries: the descent into hell; Christ's reaching into the bowels of the earth; going down among the dead, the nameless, the forgotten. We proclaim that he is raised up, but not without first going down.

Mary Magdalene stood weeping at the tomb where he had been laid (John 20:11–18). As she wept, she bent over to look into the tomb. From the posture of bending, bowing down low, she recognized Jesus standing there. From there she went to announce: "I have seen the Lord." A whole new world opens up when we are willing to bend and bow, to see from below.

☙   The honest person looks the other right in the eye. Face to face. But what we learn from the *kenosis* of Christ, as well as from those traditions in which bowing is still customary, is that to see the other rightly and to understand ourselves in relation to them, we need always to be mindful of our place. And our place is from the earth, on and in the earth, whatever may be said of our place in that new heaven and earth which is promised. Gently bowing to the other, we are reminded not so much of their superiority, but of the respect that is due each and every one, and every living creature alive in the image of God. This God is made known to us in bowing, in bending toward us in a generous descent. And it is from that vantage point that we see what a noble gesture it is to bend down before the other, boldly bowing low. Or to simply nod in respect for all those we meet, with whom we walk together down paths earthen and earthly toward the place to which Christ has ascended—God's right hand.

Earthen Tether

Grace and Connectedness

🖎 We always sat down at six sharp. The steam would seep out of my mother's ears if my father came late for dinner. She didn't like to cook, saying that she was not very good at it. But it was all we ever knew of eating, and she got better—and even grew to enjoy it—over the years. In those days we never went to restaurants. It was before the advent of fast food or the drive-by "In 'n out Burger." I remember the first time I saw a drive-in coffee shop, with teenage girls on roller skates delivering trays of burgers, fries, and milkshakes to the car window...and then retrieving the dirty dishes. This was long before paper plates and cups! I was flummoxed. I couldn't grasp the idea of bringing food to the car, let alone eating there, so tethered was I to stove, oven, and kitchen table as the venue for eating.

The meal usually lasted one full hour. Mother would ask Dad how things had gone at work. As they reviewed the day, my sister and I would make green igloos with canned peas on our plates. I always built skyscrapers with my carrots, which I hated above all other vegetables. From time to time Mother would introduce something new. My father and I were visibly horrified at the first appearance of broccoli on our table on Yocum Street. "It's fresh, just brought in today. Shut your mouth, eat the broccoli, and thank the good Lord for what's in front of you." I did shut my mouth—the broccoli never entered it until I was in my twenties.

Once, in my father's absence, Mother decided to make us oyster stew to broaden our horizons beyond tuna salad, only to watch the creamy grey soup gel in our bowls until bedtime. We would not give in. Neither would she. And so we sat. "Eat your supper before it gets cold." My refusal was, perhaps, my first and most defiant act of disobedience.

During dinner, I routinely cut into small pieces the liver my mother found so costly and worked so hard to prepare just right. As Mother and Dad became more and more focused on the problems of the day, I would hurl little chunks of liver, one by one, over my shoulder so that they would lodge behind the kitchen radiator. *This would be a wonderful treat for Ginger,* our dog, I thought. But how much harder it was to make a Ginger Snack of Campbell's Oyster Stew!

We never left the table until our father was finished with the meal. When he was finished, not just with the meal, but also with his second cup of coffee, we could then ask to be excused from the table. But there was no rushing it. This was our time together, each and every day. Suppertime was far more than the occasion for fulfilling bodily needs. There is more to food than eating. So much depends on what you do with it, how it looks, and the aroma that wafts through the house for hours before finally setting it all out on the table.

Around what was put on the table we learned about manners: please and thank you, talking and listening, serving others. We learned early on to clear the table and help with the dishes—and about the love that goes into preparing a meal and the bonding of those who eat together. And about hunger. Never, ever, was food to be wasted. Every morsel was to be finished on the plate or, *alas!* every drop drained from the bowl. As I learned through the Oyster Stew Battle, tensions at table not only cause indigestion, they also strain-to-breaking the tether that the shared meal is meant to tighten.

☙   I spoke to them of the supper table. Newly arrived in California, birthplace of McDonald's, I was trying to explain to my first class of college students the roots of the Christian Eucharist in the Passover Meal. I spoke of common plates and many cups, about passing dishes and many hands taking from them—without benefit of hygienic knife, fork, and spoon. Some wrinkled their noses at the thought. I spoke of stories told and memories forged, identities strengthened and meanings, purposes, and values instilled in us—all at table. Waxing eloquent as young professors are inclined to do, I was gently interrupted by Carol, a bright and quite pretty senior who quizzed: "What *is* a supper table?" Combing over her history later in my office, it became clear that she had no familiarity with such practices as those of my childhood on Yocum Street. Her family had no custom of a common daily or weekly meal.

🖋 "Have you eaten?" I learned to ask this question first when a visitor or traveler arrives. "Yes, I grabbed a sandwich at the airport" a familiar phrase nowadays that bespeaks a whole different mindset, a different relationship to food and to eating. We "grab" things to eat, often pre-prepared and on the move. We no longer seem to eat at set times of the day; rather, we eat when it suits us. We are busy people with cluttered and conflicting schedules. Who has the time and patience to sit down at six with everyone gathered at table? Sometimes we make the effort, but for too many of us the best we can manage is the gathering on Thanksgiving Day. For the rest, we grab things to eat and rely on others, strangers we are willing to pay minimum wage, to prepare what we eat in restaurants, "food courts," or from the frozen food section of the supermarket. Most of us have very little sense of where our vegetables are grown and have no idea where the herds which give us milk feed. We risk "dis-incarnation," uprooted from the land on which we live, unrelated to the ground from which life springs and to which our bodies will return at the end of our days.

In the Incarnation, God becomes part of the food chain. Throughout the New Testament, Jesus is depicted with food and drink. At the lake of Tiberius, after they have all eaten, Christ instructs them to go about feeding those in his flock. We are instructed to give a cup of cold water in Christ's name as a sign of our discipleship. He and his followers feed the hungry crowd with loaves and fishes. Jesus dips a morsel at the last meal with his followers. He is fed in the home of Peter. He is given vinegar instead of water to quench his thirst on the cross. All of these earthen, earthly elements are the stuff on which Jesus depends during his life among us.

We are in profound error if we hyper-spiritualize the significance of food and drink, or trivialize eating, the sign of our connection to and dependence upon the goods of the earth. Indeed, the dependence on earthen and earthly elements, perhaps more than anything else, reminds us that we are creatures. For all the grandeur and majesty of the liturgy, for all the dignity and solemnity of our worship, the whole of the sacramental life of the Church rests on four very basic elements of the earth: bread, wine, water, oil. Everything else that is said and done is to enhance rather than obscure the simplicity of these things that come from the ground and keep us linked to it, whatever we might care to say about the promise of the heavenly banquet anticipated in our celebration of the sacraments.

Water gives life, quenches thirst, refreshes, cleanses. But if there is too much, it may also drown what lives. It may take life away. All these meanings are at play when water is used to baptize into the death of Christ and new life in him. Oil soothes, heals, comforts, strengthens, and seals in moisture. And so it does when used in the sacramental life of the Church. Wine, fruit of the ground, tended, crushed, and pressed by human hands gladdens the heart, gives joy to the soul, is good for the stomach, and binds together those who partake in celebration of the promise of a future full of hope. Bread can be taken and hoarded, depriving others of basic nourishment. But it can also be given, passed around, and shared. On it we feed, giving strength to our bodies, and building our strength as one Body.

Whatever spiritual significance is attributed to the sacraments, it is the most fundamental meanings that must be kept in view. We are creatures. We are contingent beings, and like other creatures of the earth, we must eat to live. But that which makes us human, and that which humanizes us more fully, is eating together with others: sharing a meal, spending time together at table, exchanging words and hopes and dreams, the problems that must be sorted out with children, neighbors, brothers and sisters.

Perhaps one of the most important elements of Christian faith and life is held out to us with the words: "take and eat," "take and drink." In a culture of prepackaged meals and microwave cooking, of take out and grabbing a sandwich on the run or sipping Starbucks as we race down the freeway, we would do well to ponder these words and consider what is being given. Being embraced by the mystery of the Eucharist, the heart and soul of Catholic life, may require that we learn how to eat again, retrieving in our homes and households a feel for the vital necessity of sharing a meal together: chopping and dicing, stirring and stewing, pouring, waiting, setting places, sitting and facing one another, passing plates and knowing how much to take and how much to let remain for others. Then clearing and cleaning. And afterward, resting from all that tiring preparation, absorbing the words exchanged, digesting what we have received of the earth, which also serves as a reminder of that which tethers us to the ground.

℞   In my mind's eye, I see her now. No longer surrounded by family at table, she sits there alone. Every day at six sharp. She does not like fast food, packaged meals, or instant anything, even coffee. Indeed, she has grown fussier in her later years. She does not let a day go by without preparing meals her own way. "Sure, it's better when you have family to cook for. But you have to eat."

In her solitude, my mother sits at table, a modest meal set before her. No more fights over Oyster Stew; no more Broccoli Protests, no more Liver Surprises for Ginger. That meal, taken in quiet and in peace, links her to all of those for whom she cooked; to the circle of family and friends she fed for so many years. For a simple yet sage woman who has always known the importance of the body—hers and ours—it keeps her linked to the rhythm of the seasons, to the earth's wise ways. It is a simple thing: putting food in the body so that it might live and flourish. Alone or with others, it tethers us to those we love, to the food chain on which God in Christ was dependent and still depends in order to nourish us through bread, wine, water, and oil.

Of Names and Naming

Community and the Blessings of Tradition

🖎 The church was packed. They had lots of friends and family who had come a great distance for the wedding. In the long ago, people would say that this couple married late in life. They were in their mid-to-late thirties. He was a well-known musician; she quite accomplished in her own right, distinguished as a teacher and leader in the local Hispanic community. They were married in the San Francisco Bay area and drew a large number from what is often called the "S and J" crowd, those whose commitment to social justice and peace is front and center in their lives.

The wedding was wonderful. The music was superb. Prayers were offered in different languages, and the couple invited the participation of parents, brothers and sisters, nieces and nephews, and friends galore.

It was also a *long* wedding. It was hot. Everyone was sweating. There were no tuxedos, thank goodness, and no bridesmaids in peach chiffon. I was the best man, in a loose fitting, bought-somewhere-in Mexico shirt. The bride wore a free flowing dress that her sister found somewhere in Latin America, and the groom was dressed a bit like me: everything roomy and light, except for our heavy beards. Cynics would have likely commented on this rather unusual crowd: "A bunch of '60s leftovers." And so we were.

Finally, we reached that place in a wedding Mass when all breathe a sigh of relief. It's done. All the blessings have been uttered and all the promises of a lifetime rendered. We were hungry and thirsty and waiting to move on to the reception, to continue the celebration. "The Mass is ended, go in peace." "Thanks be to God." The officiating priest, who seemed very much at home, could not have known bride and groom all that well, however. If he had, he would have spared them, and himself, the embarrassment that came next.

After the dismissal, he paused and added: "May I present to you, for the first time, Mr. and Mrs. ..." The bride laughed aloud. The groom was stunned; he had never thought of her with his name...because she intended to keep her own. The crowd chuckled, in part because of the priest's *faux pas,* but just as much because of the bride's reaction. None of us would have thought for one moment that she would give up her own name and take his. It simply wasn't "who she is."

☙   What's in a name? Identity. Who we are, have been, and will become is wrapped up in the name we bear. And our name designates the kind of relationships we have with others.

There is a story to every naming, and every name has a story. Our names generally do not just drop out of the air. Parents often name a child for someone in the family, hoping not only to pay them homage, but also that the namesake will embody some of the qualities or virtues of the one whose name they bear. There is a long and noble Christian tradition of naming a newborn for a biblical figure such as Rebecca, Rachel, Ruth, David, or Daniel, or a saint such as Catherine or Charles. In some cultures the child bears the name of the saint on whose feast day the child came into the world. If your birthday is June 1, you get Justin or Justine. Some are not so lucky!

Likewise, those who embraced the vowed religious life in years past often took, or were given, a new name "pronounced by the mouth of the Lord" (Isaiah 62:2), which replaced their baptismal name. I have a distant cousin, Margaret, who had the great misfortune of being given the name "Otteran" in religious life. As a child, I had a hard time understanding why God would even think of a name like that, let alone want anyone to be called by it. Of course, I then began to think of Margaret as one of those happy sea creatures who gleefully belly-surfed down the sliding board in the pool at the Philadelphia Zoo. Taking another religious name signified leaving family and whatever social standing—high, middle, or low—that the family's name conveyed. The religious name signified a new identity with the sisters in community, with the Church, and in relation to the world.

Names and naming are power-laden. "Kennedy" opens up a whole world of meaning: family and political stances, privilege, self-sacrifice, loss, and grief. "Diana" conveys beauty, the quest for integrity, as well as tragedy. Just say the word "Gandhi" and people throughout the world conjure up images of peace and non-violence.

The name we are given and carry with us through life is not the only name we are called. From very early on, we hear ourselves referred to by other names: "Smart," "Slow," "Sissy," "Super," "Strong," "Stingy," "Spic," "Shanty Irish." While some of the names others give us help us to grow in self-knowledge, to becoming the person we are called to be, not all of them do. We must sift through the names and naming to find that which is truly ours. But we err if we think that we can name ourselves by ourselves alone. We cannot allow others to decide who we are in their naming us, but others are crucial in the discovery of our deepest identity, who we really are. To say that we do not name ourselves is to recognize that we never arrive at our true identity and purpose in life on our own. The deeper question at the heart of us all is not, "Who am I?" but rather "Whose am I?"

℞   We live an answer to this question all life long. And we answer it in the concrete decisions we make and through the specific direction we give to our lives. As we live and draw near to the answer, we do hear the sounds, or glimpse the traces, of the letters that together make up the name—the naming—that only God can give. Indeed, this is the new name "pronounced by the mouth of the Lord" (Isaiah 62:2), the one deeper than any other name and naming, spoken in the chambers of the heart, the echoes of which find their way to words that can be spoken only in the hushed murmurs of the deepest kind of prayer: "I am God's. And God is faithful."

There are names and naming throughout the Scriptures. Saul becomes Paul. Zachariah's son is called John to everyone's surprise. But the more important naming is found in the effort to speak of God, call upon God, to name God rightly. The one called Rock, Fortress, Vanguard, Hope, and Strength is, on the lips of Jesus, called "Father."

Jesus is called "Word" and "Son" of the Father. The love between them is named "Spirit."

None of these names fully discloses God's identity or tells us loud and clear, once and for all, who God is. Rather, the names and the naming are about relationship, since "Father" and "Son" are relational terms, names that designate relationship. The relationship between them is one of mutual self-gift, which is the nature of love and love-ing. "Spirit" is the name of this back-and-forth self-giving love. When God names God, the first and last word is Love. This love designates a relationship of such a kind that we too—all of us, with our different names and stories of naming—are a part.

Watching the opening of the 2004 Summer Olympic Games on TV with a group of friends, I commented on the beauty of the various peoples entering the stadium in Athens, carrying the flags of their countries. An ocean of people in that Olympiad. Looking closely I began to focus on the different colors of skin, the shapes of their bodies, their eyes and hair. Some were short, some tall and muscular; all were fit. The cameras flashed as their teeth glistened, eyes turned upward to the crowd sitting in the layers and layers of stadium seats. The noise of the crowd was near deafening. Not unlike the hoards gathered at the Super Bowl, or the thousands upon thousands ringing in the New Year at Times Square. Then there is the silent groaning of those gathered in protest in Tiananmen Square, or waiting to pass customs in the airport, or lined up in the Sudan in the hope of being fed.

Crowds. Teaming crowds, a sea of the nameless, throngs of pulsating masses. Yet each with a name. And a story. It is the name and the story of our naming, even and especially amidst the masses, that lets us know where we belong, to whom we belong. "Whose am I?" It links us to one another, to all those others of whom we are a part, now and then. Not just those with whom we live and love and serve, but with those who have gone before us. And with those yet to come, the children yet to be named, whose stories are yet to be written, which will be told in their living and then remembered.

    ☙   Away from the crush of the Los Angeles freeways, from the millions upon millions who have come to the shores of Southern California, I sit quietly in the cool open space of the new Cathedral of Our Lady of the Angels. I am alone there, no one near. At least not yet. It is very early morning, but I have already passed thousands of others on the freeway this morning as I drove to the cathedral. Drivers and passengers, going and coming from work; immigrant peoples waiting in the predawn hours for a bus, likely going to clean someone's home in the Hollywood hills or Brentwood, or returning from the late shift in some all-night diner. Each one has a name, be they from the barrio or Beverly Hills. And each one has a story.

So do these others that I look upon as I sit quietly in the cool of the cathedral. I look to them upon the tapestries that grace the walls—people of different colors, nationalities, epochs, ages; men and women, some well known and others less so, cleric, religious, lay, babies in arms and women with roses and rosaries. They are on my left and on my right, moving from the past onward to the future. I am in their midst: the saints and blesseds and those still on the way. The Communion of Saints, every one with a name and a story. I look to them and call upon each by name:

James • Charles Borromeo • Catherine of
Siena • Isaac Jogues • Joan of Arc • Barnabas •
Jane Frances de Chantal • Anthony Claret •
Methodius • Cyril of Jerusalem • Pius X •
Andrew Dung Lac • Aloysius Gonzaga •
Marie-Rose Durocher • Stephen of Hungary •
Matthew • Young Women of Faith • John •
Lorenzo Ruiz • Philippine Duchesne •
John Baptist Scalabrini • Joseph Vaz •
Justin • Margaret of Scotland • Helen •
Louise de Marillac • Emydius • Philip •
John Bosco • Mary of Jesus Crucified •
Francis de Sales • Philomena • John XXIII •
Mother Teresa • Bartholomew • Anselm •
Bruno • Maria de la Cabeza • Isidore the
Farmworker • John Fisher • Junipero Serra •
Mark • John Neumann • Alphonsus Liguori •
Bede • Agnes • Andrew Kim Taegon •
John Vianney • Martin of Porres • Boniface •
Justin de Jacobis • Children of God •
Bridget of Sweden • Vincent de Paul •
Bernadette • Elizabeth of Hungary •
Ambrose • Gregory the Great • Juan Diego •
Martin of Tours • Teresa of Avila •

Alojzije Stepinac • Jacinta • Patrick •
Francis Xavier • John Chrysostom •
Frances X. Cabrini • Young Men of Faith •
Jerome • Rose of Lima • Lucy • Blaise •
Anthony of Padua • Martha • Philip Neri •
Timothy • Benedict the Black • Luke • Lucia
Khambang • Perpetua • Felicitas • Andrew •
Peter Claver • Bonaventure • Andre Bessette •
Elizabeth of Portugal • Elizabeth Ann Seton •
Mothers and Children of Grace • Paul • Peter •
Charles Lwanga • Maria Goretti • Agatha •
Miguel Augustin Pro • Lawrence • Louis
Ibaraki • Paul Miki • Therese of Lisieux •
Jurgis Matulaitis • Bernard • Augustine • John
the Baptist • Maria Venegas • Peter Chanel •
Thomas • Monica • Clare • Francis of
Assisi • Joseph • Ann • Mary Magdalen •
Dominic • Nicholas • Thomas More •
Kateri Tekakwitha • Moses the Ethiopian •
Paul Chong Hasang • John Baptist de
la Salle • Maximilian Kolbe • John of God •
Katharine Drexel • Thomas Aquinas •
Bernardine of Siena • Frances of Rome • Ignatius
of Loyola • Casimir • Stephen • Cecilia •

☙   In the quiet of our room or in the tranquility of an empty church, in the doze of a nap or during the length of a long stroll, we find a space away from the crush of the crowd. We arrive at a place where we can drink from a spring called "memory," discovering refreshment in that never ending stream named "hope." Pausing between memory and hope, we hear once more the story of our naming. That name—pronounced in, through, with, and for Love alone—lets us know that we can find our way through the crowd, and will always be welcome in that House whose name is Belonging.

Too Much Red

Teaching and Learning the Way of the Heart

☞ I blame it on the hype of Christmas, the season of God's love become a marketing frenzy. It passes in the blink of an eye. The tree is taken down, we are back to the humdrum with our resolutions for the New Year already giving way to more practical considerations. There is a darkness that sets in during those first months, a heaviness in the sky as the exhaustion of late winter begins to melt into spring. April may be the wettest month, but February inflicts its own lashing: all that red! It begins creeping into the shops as soon as the Christmas merchandise has been cleared from the floor. In drugstores, grocery stores, department stores, and, above all, in the greeting card stores. Red everywhere. Red hearts, red Cupids, red arrows, red boxes with red ribbons. Inside the red boxes are chocolates with red cherry centers wrapped—surprise!—in shimmering red foil!

We have passed from the season of the Incarnation of God's love in the Word and Spirit. Yet, rather than relish the gift a bit longer, we are now urged to give Valentine's Day cards and candies to express our love and care for our sweetheart and, lately, to all our friends and co-workers, too. I demur, and, what is more, I resist the criticism that I am a curmudgeon because I do so. My resistance is rooted in a deeply felt conviction that I should not let the image of the heart be trivialized, allowing such a rich symbol to be associated simply with emotion, with fluffy feelings, with pink pitter-patter that cannot stand up to the costliness of a love that endures even when it must go through the motions in hope of better times.

☞ It plays in our minds and indeed in our souls as a symbol of love: the heart. But of what love does it speak? In the Old Testament, the words *leb, lebab,* and in the New Testament, *kardia,* convey not simply feelings of tenderness and intimacy, but, rather, they refer to the deepest dimensions of the self, so deep that it can be said that the person does not simply have a heart, but *is* the heart!

"Heart" is a way of speaking of our openness to be in relationship to another, others, and God. It is that deepest dimension of the self which is open and able to be touched from the outside and drawn toward and for the other, out of oneself, beyond oneself so that we can move onward and upward. If the heart has become the symbol of love, it is just as much a symbol of hope. Heart images what is deepest in us, and because there is nothing deeper in human life than hope, hope springs from the heart.

That which is deepest in us needs direction. On its own it can lose its way. The terrain is roomy, wide, and wonderful, but care must be taken along the way, especially with those with whom we walk the ways of love. Indeed, we can wind up moving in the wrong direction together with those with whom we have locked hearts. The heart must be taught, formed, schooled in love. But we must begin at the beginning. And the first and last lesson is one of hope, the hope within us that looks forward and is open to what lies ahead.

✒ There were 125 boys in my first grade classroom. Our teacher was Sister Mary Regina Loretta, I.H.M, perhaps in her very early twenties. We may have been her first class of first grade boys. The images of that year are still crisp and clear: the schoolyard, the blackboard, the times-tables, the perfect Palmer penmanship alphabet posted above the board, the May Procession, and making my First Holy Communion under the tutelage of my beloved teacher. My warm and fond memories of her are rekindled each Christmas when I visit her in her "active retirement."

Memories of interacting with classmates are in shorter supply, for introversion and shyness can carry a heavy price. But there is one. Indelible. Each day she gave us "seatwork." After assigning us a task to complete at our desks—in silence, of course—Sister would go to her desk to do who-knows-what. Perhaps she was marking our tests, filling out attendance sheets, or simply trying to straighten her supplies.

The memory: after giving the class its seatwork assignment, she came down the aisle and whispered to me: "Mr. Downey." (In those days even first graders where addressed in such a manner.) At first

I thought I was being chided. My fear gave way to shock as she asked, "Would you please be so kind as to go to that empty desk in the front of the room so that you can help those boys with their seatwork?" That was my first personal contact with Sister. Until then, I was not sure that she, or any of the 124 boys in the room, knew that I was there.

What help the others needed I do not recall. In retrospect, I hope that I was not showing them how to solve math problems. My true colors in the fields of math and science came to the fore in the fifth grade. The boy who had brought home honors until then came home with a big red 65 = F on his report card. And although this was the first time, it was not the last. In fact, in order to graduate from Villanova University many years later, even those majoring in the liberal arts had heavy requirements in both math and the "hard sciences." I barely survived my senior year by enrolling in a course that the School of Science called "Physics for Poets." Even at that, I had a hard go of it.

℘   But in those early school years, I did not seem to struggle as much. Learning, even the rigorous discipline of it, was a delight. As much as I enjoyed school, however, I lived for the weekly evenings at Mr. Lafferty's house, where people from all over the neighborhood would assemble for Irish dancing lessons. The room was shrouded in the blue-grey veil of cigarette smoke, discoloring the Irish flags which hung like drapes all around the room. The floor was dark hardwood, and the music was that of a live accordion, tin whistle, and fiddle. White-headed Sean Lafferty, wearing a dark three-piece suit with watch fob glistening from his vest pocket as if to draw the eye to his fat tummy, sat in the chair puffing away. His pipe tobacco was almost sweet amidst the rancid smoke of Chesterfield, Pall Mall, Lucky Strike, and Camel cigarettes. He looked us over. He surveyed the goings-on.

Little girls practiced their step dancing or jigging, following Mr. Lafferty's directions as best they could: "Back straight; shoulders back; eyes forward." The elders in the crowd sat with arms folded, one foot gently patting the floor to the rhythm of the Irish instruments and to the dancing shoes tapping on the hardwood floor. During those long evenings of lilt and laughter I danced somewhere between the jigs and the reels. Lafferty called me over to him once and reminded me: "This is not American dancing. You're Irish and this is Irish dancing. Keep your legs stiff, boy. The legs stiff."

My favorite reel was called the "Siege of Ennis," even though I heard it as the "Sea of Venice" and wondered why the Irish would name one of their very best dances for a place in Italy with its own kind of music and its own kind of dancing. When it came time for the "Siege of Ennis," most everyone in the room rose to their feet. There were no onlookers now, save Lafferty, surveying from his chair. Forming lines facing one another, young and old, stout and slender, we all joined hands. Line to line, we locked hands and raised arms high, poised for the first note. And begin! Line faces line, back and forth, face to face, now forward, now back. The music buoyed us. It was February, but the sweat poured out of our pores. Hearts pumped, breath was heavy—some with smoke. Feet lifted and were lifted from the ground effortlessly. We carried one another in the rhythm that carried us.

And then Lafferty from his chair: "Now side to side; again side to side. Again back and forth and *under* and *up!* Easy now. Back and forth; now side to side. Face forward; look ahead. Keep your eyes off your feet. Dee de le dee; dee de le dee; dee de le dee dee dee." Now caught up and captured by the dance, Sean Lafferty rang out again: "Back and forth, now *under* and *up* and *forward*," and rising with huge effort and great gusto to take his place, he joined hands, lifted his arms with all our lot as we moved forward, now to a tune we knew by heart without ever hearing a word.

℣   Long before we speak, we move. There is a rhythm to life, to the seasons, to the body, to the spirit. We know that when primitive peoples prayed or praised, they did so by dance. These days, our prayer is often word-laden. We praise God from "north of the neck." When we are schooled in the ways of worship, we learn of rubrics and responses, are instructed when to stand, sit, and kneel, and, occasionally, and only with the greatest reluctance, led to a tolerable dance which, some are quick to remind, is not part of the worship itself.

Our teaching and learning are also often "north of the neck." But the best of teachers know that, no matter what the subject matter, education is first and finally about the heart. It is not simply aimed at the head, addressing the student's intellectual capacity, transmitting information about dates, facts, figures, or the rules of grammar. Nor is it primarily to better equip the student to use the hands with this or that skill. Rather, the true teacher, the real educator, even while communicating information or training students with certain skills to earn a living, is one who discerns the rhythms in the life of the student, a rhythm that springs from and gives direction to the livingness of a student.

From its Latin roots, to educate is "to call forth." But what is it, precisely, that the teacher calls forth? It is the rhythm that springs from the deepest dimension of the person, from the heart, the place in us—which is not a *place* at all—that needs to know that the ways of life, and the spiritual life no less, are forward and back, up and down and under, then forward again. Educating the heart is aimed at allowing the student body—and the student's body—to be seized by the rhythm of hope.

The seeds of my calling were sown, unwittingly, by two teachers. It was not so much by the content of what was taught, though gratitude for that endures. It was more a manner, a way of being. Sister Regina Loretta was warm and wonderful. Like a mother hen wrapped in yards of blue and white and black, she drew near one shy baby chick among 125 and called "teaching" forth. Mr. Lafferty, instead, sat back and observed, surveying from the sidelines in an over-stuffed chair until the last moment, when he rose to his feet and joined, hand in hand and arm in arm, those who had come to learn how to dance. At a late hour, he moved back and forth, side to side, up, under, and forward, staying with his students until the end.

Lafferty taught us this too: when the reel's course had been run and we passed over and under and forward toward one end of the dance floor, when we bumped up against the wall or found that there was no more room in which to dance forward, in that dance called the "Siege of Ennis," all those who had joined hands and locked arms turned around and did it again. Up against the wall, those who were lined together, shoulder to shoulder, found a way once more, back and forth, up and down, and under and forward, together.

✒ In my mind's eye, the classroom is full. They are my students. I am their teacher. Many of them look at me as if I were the new acquisition in the zoo. Listening to me drone on about matters of God and of the heart, some are desk-dozing. I don't blame them. Sometimes we teachers, this one included, should learn to keep quiet, listen to the way we speak and to what we say. Much of it would put us to sleep, too.

In my dream, many of them are there, those I have taught over the course of twenty-five years. It is Mr. Lafferty's room, but he is long gone. The Irish flags have been taken down and the walls are now exposed. All green. The color of hope. As the students line up, I see each one of them, some more talented than others, but that does not much matter. They are poised, hand in hand, arm in arm, toe to toe, face to face. The music is throbbing. I do not know the name of the song. And I do not know the moves of this dance. But I can feel the rhythm. And that is enough. More than enough.

It is I who must now rise from the chair. I do so with such delight, joining my hands to theirs, raising my arms locked to theirs, moving to the sound of the voice whose way I am to follow now—back and forth, side to side, up, down, under, and forward—hope's dance.

Liquid Mercy

Healing and the In-Breaking of Gratitude

🖎 "No more crocodile tears!" My second grade teacher was firm. We were 121 boys in that classroom. Billy McGee sat at his desk near me sobbing. At the mention of crocodiles, the liquid streamed even faster from the eyes of my neighbor—that's how those near us in the classroom were called. Eventually he stopped. The lesson that day was clear: boys don't cry. But Billy did. And so did I. *But what about crocodiles,* I wondered. Did those long, jagged-teethed creatures jumping from the tall grass into marshy, murky waters feel so hurt, like Billy did that morning, that they shed tears? As a second grader, I was puzzled about tears.

❧ Babies cry when something is wrong, and that tells us something about tears at the most basic human level. We cry when we hurt, when we are in pain. At the earliest, there is the pain the body knows from hunger or from the chafe of a wet diaper. Later, there is the painful experience of breaking a leg, or appendicitis, or pulmonary embolism. But even when young, we also know the pain of rejection, of alienation, of severed relationships, of the loss of one we love deeply. We know the pain of estrangement, of walling ourselves in and cutting off love and its source.

Tears are a very complex physical, psychological, spiritual reality. When we cry we expose the intimate and very deep relationship of body, emotion, mind, and spirit. Tears express, to ourselves and to others, all kinds of feelings and levels of experience that cannot be conveyed in mere words. Even when overwhelmed with a sense of wonder and gratitude, we say, "I'm speechless," and then, *roll 'em,* the tears. Tears speak of sorrow, gratitude, love.

℞   I see her wailing. Long black dress, veiled head and face. She stands alongside a car that has been bombed and in which the body of her dead son lies. She takes her veil and tries to dry her tears. But they will not stop. I do not know her name. But I have seen her time and again. The woman of Iraq—Anywoman, Everywoman, the weeping woman of war. Her loss, the loss of her child—any child—an incalculable loss.

Our religious traditions give ample witness to hope. Death gives way to life; the power of love prevails over all evil. We are to live in the expectation of what the death of One by violence has given us. At times preachers and teachers have too cavalierly urged the sorrowing to take heart in the joy of the resurrection. Some continue such urging. But before such joy can take hold, we must first learn how to grieve.

Sometimes the experiences of childhood, deprivations, or abuse in its many manifestations unleash tears. Such release often comes by means of a therapeutic breakthrough. Such breaking-through to levels of pain and hurt can be a gift given in the midst of our weakness and loss. Awareness of this gift is often signaled by profound weeping, marking an opening in the healing process as we move to deeper freedom and greater gratitude.

✎   The Scriptures bear witness to tears that flood from natural human emotions, but also from deep sentiments related to the experience of God's grace that affect the whole person—not just the "spiritual life." These tears arise in response to all that makes up the various movements of a life lived in relationship with God.

A woman named Mary wipes the feet of Jesus with her tears. They express her sorrow and her faith in the abundance of mercy. The well-loved *Pieta* of Michelangelo elicits such response from us, brings some of us to tears, because of the depth of the Mother's suffering. Jesus himself weeps because of Jerusalem's hardheartedness, which amounts to their refusal of God's love. Those who weep and mourn are called blessed in Jesus' Sermon on the Mount. Their tears bear fruit in joy when grace, known through God's action in our own hearts or through the kindness and care of others, prevails.

The fruits of this beatitude are manifest in unwavering hope and joy in the face of our daily trials and in times of persecution.

☞   As with most things, too much can be just as bad as too little. We need discernment when it comes to our crying. Why our tears, and from where? From an experience of sorrow because of our refusal, and that of others, in the face of the magnitude of God's love? Or do they gush from our melancholy or self-pity? And, just as important, what sort of fruit springs from the moisture of our tears? Does the well of our crying spill over in a way that drowns with sorrow everything it touches? Or does our weeping water the heart, ours and those of others, in a way that brittleness and bitterness give way to deeper bonds of intimacy: with the other, others, and God? Do our tears have their source in the love of God and bear fruit in holiness?

Christian tradition, of both East and West, understood tears as part of the spiritual life. They cleanse and purify our relationship with God and with others. There are *tears of sorrow* that spring from a profound sadness because of our estrangement from God, the pain of being lost and in the dark, the futility of clinging to the false self, the self-centered self in the face of the magnitude of God's love, manifest in giving the self away in and for love.

This love, once known, often shows itself in the *tears of intercession* for those whom we love, but who do not seem to know the abundance of God's love. Monica cried tears of intercession for her son Augustine. Today her spirit lives in the countless mothers and grandmothers brought to tears at the sight of their children and grandchildren who are lost in the ways of drug abuse, crime, addiction. They bring their tears to God and plead with God not to lose sight of those they love.

There are *tears of empathy* that gush forth at the very thought of such enormous suffering in the world: massive and senseless violence, disease, systematic oppression of peoples, which call not only for my empathy, but for communal mourning that mobilizes us to work against institutionalized injustice and to live in solidarity with the poor of the earth, the weak and the wounded in society and Church.

And then there are the *tears of helplessness* that roll down our cheeks when we remember those in our families and others we love whose lives seem to be disintegrating right before our eyes, and we can do nothing. We are utterly powerless to save them from their own self-destruction brought on by rage, arrogance, pride, self-absorption, and self-pity. We commend them to God's mercy and trust that the never-ending current of our tears carry them there.

☞ "I can't cry." Of all the things she said of herself, this was the most intimate. Ours was a most unusual exchange. I had always found her a bit reticent. It's not that she was forbidding or frightening...just somewhat reserved. At the same time, she struck me as splendidly childlike. She would say what she had to say in the simplest of terms, in the way in which a child can describe things as if they are self-evident: out of the mouths of babes. She spoke this way about the things of God, too.

She had been serving long as the Reverend Mother of a good-sized community of contemplative nuns. Not only had she invited me to give the nuns a week of conferences, she also welcomed me more warmly and graciously than I had expected. To boot: she actually seemed quite interested in my talks, which came as a surprise to me. I could not imagine that I might say something about the life of the Spirit that would actually be of some help to someone so familiar with its ways.

We decided to spend an hour together. The purpose: to chat. But one hour gave way to two, which in turn gave way to three. In the course of our exchange, my words gave way for hers. I suppose that even deep introverts and contemplative teachers in the ways of God need to talk from time to time. I recalled the opening word of the *Rule of Benedict*—"listen"—and so I decided that this might be an occasion for me to learn a little from a real spiritual guide. So I listened and tried to drink it in.

"I can't even cry with my sisters. Maybe one day I will." This was because of a family situation turned tragic many years ago. As a young girl, the Reverend Mother moved in with relatives who raised her with her cousins, whom she had not known well before joining their family. Away from her own home and separated from her parents and sisters, she pined for them, especially a favorite older sister with whom she remained close. When this sister married, the younger girl was thrilled. But just weeks after the wedding, the favorite sister died in a fire.

Her death altered the life of the Reverend Mother from that day forward. Unable to go to her dying sister, and sensing that the others did not understand, the younger girl hid her grief from everyone. Alone that night, she cried a river—no, an ocean—of tears. But when that night's flooding stopped, she never cried again. Unable to share this sorrow with her relatives, it joined her reservoir of collected heartache over losing home and family and so much else, and she suppressed her tears so deeply that they never broke the surface again. For most of us, the healing tears of mourning dot the course of our lives, and the Reverend Mother knew she had more to shed. She would find them...in God's own time.

When I remember the Reverend Mother in my prayer, as I remember her and each of her sisters, including the one lost in that fire, I ask for the gift of tears. I ask for this gift for us all, that our eyes be bathed in the liquid of mercy, those cleansing waters that make us squint and gaze through soothing, soft clouds of aquamarine. At first, we are overwhelmed when we've cried so forcefully. We cannot catch our breath, like the child who cries so hard it seems as if she has forgotten how to breathe. Then, after who knows how long, we breathe in an unfettered freedom whose anthem is gratitude for the abundance of God's mercy shimmering all around us.

❧   I dream that we are all singing now. I am singing, as is the Reverend Mother, at last bathed in tears of gladness. There is the newly-married sister now long laid to rest, and all the sisters in the monastic choir. We are joined by the mother whose daughter has gone wrong, whose grandson is plagued by illness and addiction; the father who lost his son long ago in Vietnam; the woman of war in Iraq; and the brother who laments quietly day and night because there is nothing more he can do to bring those he loves closer to the healing and the life that comes by turning to God's love and mercy and asking for help. The first line of our song is there in the Psalms, number 126. All together now: "Those who sow in tears shall reap rejoicing."

Courage to Cross

Faith and the Costliness of Fidelity

🐦 Benjamin Franklin and Walt Whitman. One a thinker, an inventor, the "Father of Electricity." The other a dreamer and the poet of *Leaves of Grass* fame. Franklin is Philadelphia's finest local, though some natives would cast their vote for Grace Kelly, the late Princess of Monaco. Whitman, barely mentioned in most renderings of U.S. history, is one of the great literary voices of his own time. Raised in Philadelphia, I was weaned on the legends of Ben Franklin; Camden's Walt Whitman was not in the picture. Neither was that other world of "Jersey," the place across the river where he was laid to rest.

Two great men, both with bridges that bear their names. The Ben Franklin spans the Delaware River, connecting the heart of Old Philadelphia near Betsy

Ross's House and Independence Hall with Camden, New Jersey, home of Campbell's Soup, birthplace of RCA, and gravesite of Walt Whitman. The Walt Whitman stretches over the Delaware just a few miles to the south, linking South and Southwest Philadelphia with points in South Jersey, the connector for Philadelphians wending their way to the seashore resorts of Atlantic City, Wildwood, and Ocean City.

Though Philadelphian through and through, and proud of it, you might say I was "born on the wrong side of the bridge." Stories of kites, keys, and lightning, harnessing energy and signing the Declaration of Independence paled for me when set alongside Walt's *Leaves*. Early, I was taken by the power of words to bridge worlds: this one and that; here and there; there and here; you and me.

℘   I remember my first bridge crossing, what seemed to me the journey of a lifetime. My father had finally earned enough money to bring his family on vacation. Our first. One week in July at Wildwood by the Sea. We might have just as well been going cross-country as from Philadelphia to the

Jersey Shore! Loaded into my father's first car, with sandwiches and snacks and drinks for the longest journey we had ever taken—sixty-five miles—I was petrified as we neared it: *the bridge*. We had to cross the bridge.

I had heard stories of people falling or jumping, crashing into the water that seemed to be as distant from us as heaven from earth (or hell!). I can still name the fear: we would have an accident on that bridge and plunge to our deaths. Or, glued to other cars in traffic as the huge span opened to let the boats beneath pass through, ours would be the single car that would tip over the edge, nose-diving into the muddy Delaware: a deep, dark, cold, and filthy underworld.

I closed my eyes as we approached the tollbooth on the Philadelphia side. I could hear my father's description of how Irish immigrants built the bridge. He spoke of its height and weight, the length of its span. My mother's voice quivered with fright: "Keep your hands on the wheel and your eyes on the road and close your mouth!"

Getting over that bridge was an excruciating journey. But there was no other way.

And even now, there is no other way. Sooner or later we have to get past it: the terror and fright as we approach our bridge, that place in our world that we must cross over, despite fearing how long the fall might be into the abyss that threatens us. We must show up for the crossing nonetheless: close our eyes, hold our breath, and, yearning to breathe in the air of peace that awaits on the other side, we must pass through that costly tollbooth, holding on tight. And even then, the journey is not yet over. There is deeper water ahead, longer crossings still.

℞ She was almost always with us: Christmas and Easter, birthdays and anniversaries, holidays and Saint Patrick's Day. My maternal grandmother also came with us to the shore year by year. She loved to sit on the beach and sun herself, putting her feet in that cold, dark sea. "The salt water cures you," she always said in that thick Ulster buckle of a brogue. She would look on it long: to the sea. I would ponder her melancholic gaze as she looked out over that deep, across that distance to a time and place I had only heard of: High Glen. In the County Donegal, in the northwesternmost part of Ireland,

High Glen had hills so dark they seemed purple with cold, and a seashore so jagged and water so frigid that the locals dared not swim. That's why, ever after, she put only her feet in the sea.

At the time of her leaving High Glen, all the neighbors had come to the house to bid farewell to the young Mary Ann Boyce. She was departing in the early morning to go to America. The night had been full with fiddle, tin whistle, and whiskey; the morning air soaked with the sobs of a daughter ripped from her father's side. Even now my far-away family in Ireland tells of the screaming in the darkness of a night giving way to morning.

She had to be pulled away from him. She did not want to leave him for that ship that would carry her across the ocean to Philadelphia to begin again, to start a new life, to send money to bring her sister and cousins to a new world of possibility.

The way from High Glen to Philadelphia was riddled with fear and marked by a deepening sense of distance that began with that leaving. No crossing back could ever erase it. It is said that her father went to the top of the hill near High Glen and, knowing the hour of its passing, his eyes followed her "coffin ship" until it passed out of view. It was his last glimpse of her, and she never saw him again.

Beholding her wistfulness as she gazed out across that sea, I understood that the ocean is arrogant and unyielding, a place reminding us of unfathomable distance, a distance that cannot be measured even by the vastness and openness of its seas.

Even though her father was gone, eventually she did cross back again, to bring us "home." She took us to High Glen to show us the place of our origins. Though she never saw her father again, her heart was filled with happiness over being rejoined to other family and friends. Because we had crossed that depth and distance, we, too, were welcomed into that wide circle of celebration and song, knowing this place to be our home as well.

❧ My grandmother crossed over to High Glen several more times, and for the last time in her early seventies. It was not long thereafter that she went into a deep and was separated from us by a distance that was more unfathomable than the widest sea. I would gaze into those eyes that had once cherished me and now saw not the wide and warm expanse of an enfolding sea of love, but layers of a grey sky that love's sharpest, warmest ray could not probe. The space was named dementia, the hardening of the arteries to the brain. Today it is called Alzheimer's. The distance grew wider and wider, the darkness deeper and deeper. Again and again, it was I who had to initiate the crossing over—over that distance and deep, hoping that on the other side of that place there would be a lush land, still soaked with love. Smiling through tears, as I knew she herself had done again and again while crossing over, I gazed across the distance and into the depth of those empty eyes, wondering if she might cross back to us just one more time.

Indeed, she did have one more crossing, but of *this* crossing we do not know much. We learn only a little of it from being near those who have gone before us—across that distance. For the final journey, she was not ripped away from her father's arms, torn from her father's heart and home. Nor was it she who took the first step in that journey of leaving on one quiet afternoon in October. Instead, it was the Father's love that came to claim her, snatching her hand quietly, and crossing with her at the end of life's journey into the country of mercy. All other crossings were to ready her for this final journey.

℘ Our final crossing is from here to there, from what we have to what we long for. It is from what we see to what we hope for. To be joined again to our deepest love. To be reunited. To be brought into communion. To live in love without end—or beginning. No matter how wide the sea, whatever the distance, however long the journey, and no matter how many other crossings in the course of our living, in the end we all cross over to the place we long for, whose name is Love alone.

Yet, before our final crossing, we must pass often from where we are to where another is, sometimes over belligerent and antagonistic seas. We journey from self-fixation, self-absorption, self-preoccupation through the liquid of love to the soothing sands of another to whom we give our life, our very self. When our self-gift is accepted, the crossing seems worth all the effort. But the crossing must be made even—and especially—when we are not accepted by the other in love. Even then, we set out over and over...with pardon. Otherwise, it is our sorry lot to remain on the lonely shore of self, never setting out, never living, but instead languishing on the parched terrain of a dried-out, dusty heart.

🖎   We cross paths with many others every day, sometimes hardly noticing their faces as we race through the journey of life. We step out of line often enough, crossing boundaries that we know we should not, disrespectful of the dignity of others. When they are crass or coarse with us, we become coarse in turn. And a circle of anger, hatred, and cruelty continues. We can't seem to get out; we can't fly free. How to move forward over the gaps, holes, chasms, abysses we find here and there on the journey?

Indeed they can be found in our own living rooms, in our homes, our communities, in the Church, in the neighborhood. We feel their presence most when they widen in our relationships with family and friends. "We have just grown in different directions," one spouse says of the other. "Our values are so different," the brother says of his sister. The same is writ large in the wider world where nation, race, land, and language divide rather then unite. The chasms cannot be crossed with idle chatter. And if they are left alone, they split wider and wider.

The only way to the other side is for me to make the first move, to be the one to begin crossing the distance from here to there, making the move across the fluid expanse of unrestricted forgiveness. The distance between the hardened heart and the drenched marshes of mercy's enveloping shores cannot be overcome if I think that everyone else must make the first move.

The distance *will* be infinite until I take the first step. I must approach if I am to cross over. Over and over again. I must do so especially when it is I who have been wronged by the other. What happens person-to-person provides the key to crossing wider and longer spans between one nation and another, from one race, class, or culture to another, amidst a world so deeply divided.

❧ Jesus, the true Mediator, the only one called "priest" in the New Testament (Hebrews 4:4–5:10), became a bridge between time and eternity, laying himself down as the Way for our crossing to God. All who are baptized into the Body are to make bridges of their bodies as Jesus did. Bridge building is the task of the whole Christian community, so that together we become a road to reconciliation and peace. We need the courage not settle the score, but to build the bridge, to make the journey, to cross over. The gaping silence of enmity must give way to the sounds of sorrow and pardon.

"Which of you has not sinned?" You? Me? Then go ahead and throw that stone, plucked from the rubble that surrounds us, often of our own making. Along the journey, I have picked up stones of hurt and resentment, rage and fury, and have held on to them as if for life itself. But to live while gathering stones as weapons is to live in a place foreign to the wide and wondrous expanse which is the heart's true home.

Rather than keeping our stones ready for throwing, we can use them to build. Bridges. To get from here to there. Across rivers and seas so wide and deep they appear forbidding. Not only must we cross, we must be the connectors, building the bridge that will heal the disparate and fragmented elements of our lives and the lives of others.

We must look from here to there, always gazing to the other side. There is One who has made the journey through the land of forgiveness before us, One who has crossed the deep and wide waters of pardon. Waiting now at the other side of that wide and wonderful sea, which is ours to cross, it is the One whose name is Mercy within Mercy within Mercy, whose life is the bridge from here to there. He will take us with him, but it is not ours to sit and wait. Like him, we take the first step in building a bridge with the one and only life we have to live.

Poised for Gifting

Detachment and Openness of Spirit

🖎 A confession: my relationship with sleep is strained. We are strange bedfellows. I was firstborn, and there are stories in abundance of my fighting sleep in infancy. As the only son, I always had my own bedroom, even though our house was very small. The result is that I am a "light sleeper"; I never seem to get much of it. So I look with no small measure of envy at those who can drop off and doze at the drop of a hat. Some say that easy sleep is the sign of a clean conscience. In my more mean-spirited moments, I think it signals a dull conscience—or perhaps no conscience at all! But after I sleep on it—what sleep I can manage—I see it a little differently.

❧ "I am Phaolo, Sleeping Child." He would awaken quickly and quietly, then spring to his feet. There was no stretching or yawning, but the sleep was deep. Whenever we all piled into the car, boarded the plane, settled into our place on the train, Phaolo would, in mere minutes, lean back and sleep like a log, drifting off into the "sleep of the dead" until our arrival. He seemed effortlessly sustained between the two states of being awake and being asleep. Like so many other Vietnamese, Phaolo works long and hard. Sleeping a few hours at night and then intermittently throughout the day, his is a life lived between waking and sleeping.

❧ Ours is a culture of sleep deprivation. Studies show that most of us do not get nearly enough. Could this, in part, explain the short tempers, road rage, and general lack of patience with one another? Loud-mouthed, ring-reader-like advertisers on television promise us a good night's sleep, "Or your mattress is *free!*" But we know in our depths that there are likely much deeper reasons than a mattress for the bone-tiredness we carry, for those seemingly endless, sleepless nights.

Sleeplessness has many causes, some quite complex. But too often, in the ordinary round, our fretting, our tensions, and our worries bring on sleeplessness. We are anxious. We are kept awake by those tapes—now CDs!—replaying certain events of our lives over and over again in our heads. Our regrets and resentments, our attempts to settle the score or get our way hold us captive—all alone, in the dark, while the rest of the world sleeps.

There is something healing about sleep. "Nature's balm," is how the nurse described it after I had to undergo emergency surgery, adding, "Wasn't that what Shakespeare called it?" Shakespeare or not, the nurse had enough homespun wisdom to know the soothing quality of sleep. The body slows down; the system is given a chance to find some balance after the invasive shock of surgery or the insult of illness. When sick or in the hospital, a crucial ingredient in the prescription for wellness is sleep. As much as possible.

☞   Jack goes to visit his mother every day. Faithfully. There are days when he goes two or three times to see her. Following the death of his father, he had tried to care for her himself, and managed to do so for more than two years. But when dementia caused her to wake and dress in the middle of the night, to begin setting the table for breakfast at 2:00 A.M., he knew that he could no longer do it alone.

When she first went into the nursing home, they would walk around the rose garden outdoors or relish their favorites from a big box of See's Candies. But gradually, her greater need became sleep's embrace. These days I ask him once or twice a week: "How is your mother, Jack?" It's usually the same: "sleeping." In recent months, when I have made a trip to see her, I leave with a slight sense of disappointment. It's really no big deal, but each and every time I visit, she is...well...sleeping. So I stand and look on her, touch her forehead, whisper a little prayer. She does not budge. It is not unlike times when I quietly pause at a sleeping child's bedroom door and offer a prayer for his contentment.

🖎   Little babies sleep a good part of the night and day. As they grow, we see them begin to "fight sleep." Tired from the activities of the day, drained by the stimulus around them, their eyes begin to close as they drift off to another world. But often, the child tries with all her might to resist, to stay awake, while parents seek to soothe and settle her so that she can finally be "put down" to sleep.

Once she is "put down," I behold, I gaze, I am transfixed by the little one who has, with utter abandon, finally entrusted herself to sleep. My eyes often find rest in the movement of the small chest, that slight heaving up and down, as she takes in air and leaves the trace of her breath in the world...unselfconsciously, effortlessly.

When there is movement—the wrinkling of the nose, the fluttering of the eyelids, a slight jolt in the body as it sleeps—we sometimes say that a baby is "dreaming about the angels." We do not know what is happening as the little one sleeps; most of us cannot remember that far back. But dreams and angels go together as far back as we can remember. In the Bible, angels are messengers. And messages come in dreams.

Pharaoh looked to Joseph to help him figure out his dream, which launched Joseph into a favorable position while in captivity in Egypt. Jacob falls asleep and dreams of angels and ladders, up and down, perhaps tossing and turning as he wrestles with an angel whose blessing he seeks. Joseph betrothed to Mary dreams of "first the bad news then the good news" that she pregnant and, though he has every right to do otherwise, he knows he is to provide protection for both the mother and child. And there is the wife of Pilate, whose dream hints at the forbidding consequences of the decision her husband is about to make. Despite the dream's power, she cannot persuade him to turn back from his course.

℘ When we sleep and dream, we give ourselves over to another way of being. Day in and day out we are usually quite busy. There are things to be done from rising to washing to preparing breakfast, getting to work, the seemingly endless tasks that make up the day's labor, and then returning home where there are yet more things to do. We live in an age of assessments and outcomes, five-year plans and measurable goals. Many of us have become "doers unto death." There is so much to be done that we are inclined to think of ourselves primarily in terms of our work, what we do. Often on meeting someone for the first time, on learning their name, we no longer ask, "How do you do?"; rather we ask or we are asked, "What do you do?" In the midst of so much activity, we might do well to stop for what one of my Irish cousins calls "a big fat sleep." And then, to think long on this: "If you are what you do, then when you *don't,* you're *not!*"

"Nature's balm" may or may not be Shakespeare's, but sleep is most certainly a gift from God to those who live amidst such frenzy brought on by the mounds of things to do, who are surrounded by endless chaos and confusion. Raucous, nerve-rattling music is pumped into our ears even in bookstores. All the "stuff" in department stores, grocery stores, and Wal-Mart Super Centers reminds us that, whatever our prayer might be, we bow to the stimulating icons of materialism and consumerism: "Thy Thing-dom come."

☙   Striving to live for Kingdom rather than Thingdom, the committed celibate's real poverty and nakedness is seen in the bedroom, in bed. The celibate sleeps alone and, in so doing, enters into incarnate union not with the spouse, but into solidarity with the poor, the weak, the wounded; the last, littlest, and least in society and Church, the poor of the earth who have nothing of this "Thingdom," but whose greatest poverty is that they have no one. They sleep alone.

Those in love "sleep together" by making love. When love is made, love is made nude. Each has nothing, save the body, and all the love a heart can give. And receive. Something seems amiss when, after making love, one cannot sleep; when, having given of oneself in the act of love, one cannot abandon oneself into the arms of the other and into the restoration of sleep.

When we sleep, we let go. We release our grip and the body is loosened of its preoccupations and tensions, and the mind, the psyche, relaxes. We are not active in our sleep, or at least we are not *doing*. The clothing of the day is shaken off, the makeup is cleansed from the face, and jewelry is put away until the morrow, the eyeglasses set to the side. It is *me* in that bed, without pretensc or defense. I put myself down in a posture of vulnerability and powerlessness. There, in the various postures of rest and sleeping, I am poised to let come to me what is to be given: refreshment, rejuvenation, healing, dreams, messages and messengers of love. It is a bold act of hope to not "fight sleep," but to put ourselves down so as to rise in the morning with all that has been given in the night. There is color in sleeping, and texture, sound, shape, movement, and feelings we cannot or will not feel or express in our waking. We breathe effortlessly, our body is replenished without effort, our spirit is soothed, indeed softened.

❧   "You'll sleep when you're dead." So my father told us as he roused us from bed on the first day of school when we'd have rather stayed tucked in or, more often, when I feigned exhaustion in the early stages of a house chore I loathed—mowing the lawn or vacuuming the rugs. Early on, the impression was forged: living is awakening; dying is sleeping or falling asleep.

We put someone into the earth, down into the ground, at the end of their life, commending them to God and to a final resting place. But before doing so, we ask God to grant them, and all who have died, eternal rest. We pray that the angels will greet them in paradise, the same "dream angels" who bring messages to the sleeping figures of the Bible.

Although praying that the deceased may find eternal rest, still we wonder about what happens after death. Being a very active people, we are inclined to consider, if only occasionally, what "activities" heaven will offer. What shall we "do" there? The answer is an emphatic "absolutely nothing!" We shall be at rest, indeed "asleep" for all eternity.

Not a few Christian theologians have treated eternal life in terms of beatific vision or blissful seeing. And, as with so much, we are inclined to view this in terms of what I will see, what it will be like for me to look on God with unending bliss. But the one whom we have learned to call Father, or Mother, the loving parent who gives all life, who sustains and protects it, who counts the hairs on the head of the child and does not forget the sparrow, is the One who eternally looks upon the child, gazes upon each child, with delight. It is ours to allow ourselves to be gazed upon by God, to be looked upon with love by Love itself. It is this that we learn in the deeper movement of prayer and even in our sleeping. So that awake or asleep we are poised to be gifted in the presence of the One who gives to the beloved, even in sleep (Psalm 127:2).

Standing Still

Expectant Prayer and the Seasons of Desire

☞   The Abbey church is barn-like in its simplicity. Clear windows allow streams of sunlight to caress the burnt sienna tile floor, to kiss the monks' choir stalls. Some afternoons I just sit there for an hour or so, watching the play of light in the church as shadowed patterns slowly make their way from one side of the church's interior to the other. If I had all day, I would just sit and watch. But I have come away to this monastic community for rest and rejuvenation. And part of that entails entering the community's rhythm of work and prayer, becoming immersed in their cadence as much as possible. And monks do not just sit through the day praying or watching the daylight making love to the stark white walls of a monastic church.

At evening, there are no more patterns at play on the walls. There is only candlelight. She is there. So are we, all facing forward, looking to her. We call her "Seat of Wisdom at Mepkin." Mary holds the Child on her lap. The Christ Child looks out, gazing upon the monks who gather seven times a day to pray in this church. This bronze statue is as sturdy as the shoulders of the monks who have given their lives to work and prayer at Mepkin Abbey near Charleston, South Carolina. Mepkin—a plantation become Trappist monastery—a word that likely means serene and lovely.

This evening I wait in silence alongside the others. All the monks are still, feeling her near in the darkness. She is the woman who waits; the Mother who prays. We look. She, too, is still—the Sorrowful Mother who did not speak but who, when the time came, simply stood at the foot of the cross of the Child-become-the-Crucified One. Then she did not clutch or cling; and still she does not demand. She ponders, holding all the pain and hurt and suffering one heart can know.

We look to her and chant the words that have rolled down the ages: "O clement, O loving, O sweet Virgin Mary." She is tender; she is strong. She is a woman of courage and of faith. She listened long and lovingly to the Word of God, perplexed and puzzled, yet poised in freedom of spirit to say "yes." At the close of day we greet this woman of the dark: *"Salve."* Darkness is the very soil of hope. From it the light springs. In the beginning it was all there was; and God was there, in the darkness.

We are still. She waits with us, for us, in the darkness and stillness even as we leave her and put ourselves to bed. The Word she welcomed stirs within us; the Spirit hovering over her breathes in us even in our sleep. She waits until we rise to wait yet again for the God who comes. She is open. Expecting. Anticipating the Word made flesh in her—the Seat of Wisdom at Mepkin.

We must wait as she did so that the Spirit of God might overshadow our life, too; our bodies, tired yet hopeful, penetrated by the Word. So we stand still, waiting and wanting all the while. When we pray deeply—from the inside out—this is just what we do, which is, in fact, doing nothing.

❧   I have a hard time praying, except for all the time—that deep and sustained contemplative awareness that leads to a sense of praying at all times. This is God's gift that allows "praying always" to really be possible. We are inclined to think of praying in terms of what is said and done during set times of the day or the week. But prayer of the deepest kind is not confined to specified times, places, and words. Because prayer is rooted in desire, and desire never leaves us.

What do you want? What do you yearn for so deeply you can taste it? The kind of wanting that makes your body throb with desire. The kind of wanting that governs you, takes over, drives you, makes you near crazy for it! What is the desire that makes you hot? The yearning you live for? If truth be told, its focus changes, but desire itself is always there. If it is not, then something has gone terribly wrong.

And yet, desire has its seasons. At times we are hot, enflamed; other times we are breezy, almost cool, in our desire. We want in degrees, and there are different kinds of wanting. Sometimes we want something so much we say: "It's to die for!" But wanting knock-your-socks-off chocolate cake is very different than wanting to see a child live and thrive. Or the ache for the love of the one we love—the kind of wanting that makes you believe you are bleeding, it hurts so bad. Indeed, when we are left alone, we want to know where the one of our loving has gone. We check the weather wherever they might be, wanting to know if we both look to the same stars even while apart. At times we can catch the scent of the one we love long after they have gone—even when they have gone before us in death. We want them that badly.

When we love, what we want more than anything else is to spend time with the one we love: to draw near, to get up close, to gaze upon the beloved, to be looked upon by those eyes, to draw from the breath of the other, to breathe in unison with the one we love. We want to be filled with the life and love of the other, to be filled so much that we cannot hold any more. And then, by being filled to the bursting point, we find that there is yet more room in us for having been broken by this love. What we want is the very life of the other: the beloved, whole and entire. But we know that the only way to the heart of the beloved is to give all the love and all the life we have...to the other of our loving. This is precisely how God loves.

God's love and life—God's very self—is given, once for all, in Love that is seen, touched, and heard, Love's breath/ing at the depths of the human heart, quickening all that lives and breathes. In response to that gift, we are inclined "to do" or "to say" our response. But there is another response: the prayer of standing still, simply looking, beholding, breathing in the love of God, which is always being offered but so often ignored in our saying and doing. Prayer of the deepest kind, contemplative prayer is, above all, about seeing. But to look and to see deeply, we must stand still. As John Milton wrote, "They also serve who only stand and wait."

Sometimes prayer is dusty. Sticking with it is like suffering through a dry season that seems to never end. At other times, prayer is deeply lush and sensual, vibrant with color and texture and scents reminiscent of the sprouting of spring. Sometimes it languishes in the scorching heat of a long, sweaty summer, calling to my mind admonitions from my childhood as I squirmed in Philadelphia's humid, sticky summers: "It wouldn't be so bad if you would just stay still!"

℘   We are forever wanting. But what we want changes. It all depends. What seemed a matter of life and death—we wanted it so bad—now appears insignificant, sometimes downright silly. We can't even remember exactly what it was that we wanted, or why we wanted it so much. Desire grows and flourishes. Desire taken in the wrong direction can be deadly. It can take over our lives and the lives of others. It can kill. But the desire for God moves in another direction. It becomes what it wants: good, true, beautiful. Desire for God looks only to its own increase. It wants to keep on wanting and to be filled with this wanting of a God who is good, true, and beautiful enough to die for. God and God alone. Bernard of Clairvaux had it right: *God* is the reason for loving God.

We want it now. All of it. Whatever it might be. Results attained. Plans fulfilled. Goals achieved. Dreams come true. Skills acquired. An answer to that letter, fax, e-mail. We want our prayers answered, too. If there is no immediate answer to our prayers, then why bother? What's the point? If God does not do us good, if God does not help us out, then why waste our time and energy?

The one whose prayer takes the form of standing still waits for God even when prayers seem to go unheard and unanswered. Praying by standing still is living in the promise of presence. This presence is known deep inside from time to time. But mostly we live from hunch to hunch, hint after hint, by the whisper of a promise. We stake our life on it and continue to do so day by day. We wait to see. And we keep walking—or standing—seeking the face of God, to whom we are led in every face we see, through every longing of our hearts.

We often live with too much stuff and too much noise. Our lives are sometimes driven and divided because of the many available options. We want to have our cake and eat it too. When we learn to pray deeply, simply standing still, we cease from distraction and diversion to hear the pulse of God beating at the heart of reality, the movement of God amidst the world and within our own heart. We are still long enough to see that beneath all our wanting, at the heart of all our desire, is the desire for God—for Life,

Light, and Love—just God and God alone. This is to want it all: I want God, or at least I want to want God. Or, more modestly, as much as there is to be had of God—if God is to be had at all. And if not had or possessed, then just a glimpse of God's face, or a taste or a scent that will offer some small comfort.

At times even this much does not come, but this unfathomable and ineffable mystery—God—is still worth living for. This is precisely what one who prays standing still—however poorly amidst all the sweating and squirming—does. Praying is desiring God. Even more, praying is living in the face of the question: Who is God? We think we have the answer. But we do not yet know fully who God is. Authentic prayer searches out the answer through a whole way of life. The one who prays standing still is a living quest for God.

☞ God is at one and the same time *at hand* and always *yet to come.* The divine grace and presence overspill our beliefs and precise ideas. God is always more than we can ask or imagine. We want to pin God down, to be certain of God's nearness. But it is the gift and task of those who pray standing still to be attentive to grace loose in the world, opening eyes wide enough to search for traces of God's nearness in our own desire, our wanting, our longing, our beholding what is beautiful to look at, tasting what is good to savor, knowing what is true, and trying to do the right thing in love freely, all the while preparing for the God who comes again and again and yet again in our desiring.

Planting Year 'Round

Suffering and the Gift of Hope

🖎 After three days of driving from Los Angeles to San Antonio for a long-awaited sabbatical, I entered the driveway of my temporary dwelling. A lovely building, with an unusual parking lot in front. Waffle-like bricks made it feel almost as if I was driving over the cobblestone streets of my native Philadelphia. Tufts of grass were sticking out of the waffle-holes, a bit like brown and green Dennis-the-Menace cowlicks that couldn't be tamed.

A few days later I entered the same driveway, now with a colleague in the passenger seat. "How odd," he remarked. "The parking lot is so untidy. Look at all those patches of weeds sticking up through the driveway." Such different perceptions. Though I had not thought much about it since, the

first time I saw the Menaceing cowlicks perkily poking through the parking lot, I thought of the per-
sistence of nature, even as it strains and groans to
prevail in the most uncongenial conditions, the most
forbidding of circumstances.

☙   The thing about life is that there is so much
of it. We never get a chance to see it all at once. But
it is everywhere, in abundance. Life pours forth.
Likewise suffering. Being human means living life on
life's own terms; and this entails taking suffering into
the bargain. It seems that no one escapes. There is
the physical suffering due to illness, accident, or old
age. There is the burden of psychological and emo-
tional suffering, to say nothing of spiritual suffering.
And then there is the suffering brought on by natural
disaster: fire, flood, earthquake, famine. Perhaps
most incomprehensible of all is the suffering brought
on by humanity's inhumanity to humanity: senseless
violence, genocide, the barbarism of war, terrorism.

It is far too easy for people of faith to slough off
the horror of suffering, especially that of others, by
appealing to the inscrutable ways of God. Perhaps

even more unhelpful is the way many Christians, both in history and on the contemporary scene, compare and contrast all forms of human suffering to the magnitude of Christ's suffering on the cross. In this gruesome contest of spiritual strong-arming, humans always lose. Because no matter what the human suffering, Christ suffered more greatly still.

Such a view distorts and greatly trivializes the stark reality and excruciating pain of human suffering which, dare I say it, may be more difficult to endure than Christ's passion and death when it takes the form of the slow drip of chemotherapy over many years, or the arrival of a severely handicapped infant who will be carried by a family for most of her life, or the agony of a husband or father whose wife or daughter has been brutally raped and murdered and who cannot find the grace to forgive. The simple truth is that one day of excruciating torture and death by the asphyxiation of crucifixion cannot be compared to the myriad "crosses" that most human beings have to bear throughout their lives. Comparisons are dangerous, as are the saccharine assurances that "this too shall pass."

Often the most appropriate response is silent, compassionate presence with the person who suffers and, in hope, enduring our own suffering with the One who gave himself in self-giving love in his dying and death. This is a God who does not eradicate pain or provide clear answers to the vexing problem of innocent suffering. But this God is present in their midst. The most important practical lesson for those who live by faith: we must give up a naïve view of a God who intervenes in human affairs, filling in the gaps and wiping out innocent suffering here and now. But because Christ's suffering and death were not the final word, we cling to the hope that when our own suffering and pain is taken up in an act of self-giving, love's fruit will flower. Suffering can be redemptive if and when, in and through it, we give ourselves over in love.

Living in the presence of unspeakable suffering, we must resist the tendency to try to explain this horror in religious terms such as "God's will," "punishment for sin," or "God's inscrutable ways." This is a moment, hard as it may seem, to cling to the truth at the heart of Christian faith: God is on the side of life. We would do much better to listen, to ponder, to learn, than to allow ourselves to rush to easy answers or to get into a never-ending cycle of "why?" and "how come?"

🖎   The startling events of September 11, 2001, have made it much more difficult for us to turn our backs to the presence and power of evil in the world. Far too often we are inclined to write off the existence of evil as if it were not a real force in the world. This is no longer a responsible or realistic option. We are now confronted with our utter vulnerability. So much in our culture has clouded the truth that we are finite, we are creatures. And we are very, very vulnerable. We share a common humanity with peoples of every race and land and language. We breathe life together with every living creature. It has ever been thus. But the 9/11 events are a stark, staggering reminder of the vulnerability of our lives and the fragility of our achievements and projects: the World Trade Center's Twin Towers, eight years in the making, become a pile of rubble in a matter of hours. And this says nothing of the carnage underneath.

Amidst the ruins, we must monitor every instinct to retaliate. This instinct will surface in manifold ways, often quite unfocused and misdirected. Evil *does not win* when innocent human lives are destroyed. Evil *does win* when it gives rise to more evil. And hatred prevails only when it breeds more hatred. At the heart of the Christian faith is the conviction that in the fullness of time, the power of love will prevail over all evil. Herein lies the reason for Christian hope (cf. 1 Peter 3:15).

In these days, there is nothing more important than hope. In the coming months and years, we may find that it is in short supply. On every street, behind every other door, lives someone who is deeply disheartened, if not actually despairing. This may be brought on by the awareness of massive and meaningless death, the randomness of violence, the onset of early illness, the loss of a loved one, or job, or of one's sense of meaning and value. Or by the loss of cherished and heretofore reliable ways of thinking and speaking about our country and about God. But this loss, too, can beckon us to deeper levels of openness to hope, the kind of hope that is absolutely and altogether gift. What exactly is this gift of hope?

Hope lies at the core of all human initiative. It looks to the coming of the new, the never-before-thought-of, the unheard-of, the undreamed-of. Hope is a pregnant, many-layered reality. We can distinguish in it different shades of meaning. We can distinguish between the kind of hope we have for good weather, the cheeriness of spirit expressed in the now commonplace, "Hope you have a nice day," and something much deeper: the wholehearted anticipation of something good. In the deepest sense, hope moves us to a new perspective, enabling us to see the present in light of some future good, which we realize can only come as gift. The more difficult the circumstances in which we demonstrate hope, the deeper is the hope.

🖙 Hope is precisely what we have when we do not have something. Hope is not the same thing as optimism that things will go our way or turn out well. It is rather the certainty that something makes sense, is worth the cost, regardless of how it might turn out. Hope is a sense of what might yet be. It strains ahead, seeking a way behind and beyond every obstacle.

It is not uncommon to find that what we have put our energy into, indeed what we have staked our lives on, is unreliable. What then is our reason for hope? Can we continue in such circumstances? It is precisely when our faith is shaken and our love grows dim that hope really begins; it is in the wonder and weakness of our faith that we find hope's real meaning. Hope is the willingness not to give up precisely when we draw no consolation from what we have previously found trustworthy and reliable. Hope does not try to determine how God's ways will be shown, but remains open to new and astonishing manifestations of the divine presence. It allows something to come into life that is not of our own making. Hope is the retrieval of possibilities that come as gift.

Only in hope can we look squarely in the face of evil in the presence of the living God. This takes the greatest strength and courage, which is given to those who stand now alongside the Crucified One and with him look in hope and confidence to the life and the love of God, even and especially when the world as we have always known it seems to be crushed under the weight of hatred and violence.

Suffering and hope are related. If we suffer without hope, we become more and more resentful, angry, hateful, bitter. If we think we have hope, yet know no suffering, we are airy, naïve, living in illusion, out of touch with what is real. We must live life on life's own terms. And suffering is part of the deal.

What to do in the midst of suffering? We plant. For the sake of the children and grandchildren we sow seeds and plant trees, putting bulbs in the ground in anticipation of that day when color will spring forth and brush grey-brown hardened earth with soft yellows, purples, and pinks.

The planting must go on, everywhere and always, especially in this wintry season in the Church, amid the inclement climes of the world scene. We can never allow our creative, regenerative, fecund acts to be snuffed out by the forces that oppress and repress the human spirit, especially that suffering of the deepest kind—whatever form it takes in us. Take heart. As we continue to plant, as the seeds are sown and trees planted so that the children and grandchildren we may never see might eat, luscious ripening fruit is being born in us as we make of our own lives the seedbed of our deepest hope.

Michael Downey is Professor of Systematic Theology and
Spirituality at Saint John's Seminary and the Cardinal's
Theologian, Archdiocese of Los Angeles. Given the name
Thay Tam (Teacher of the Heart) during his time in Vietnam,
he is pictured here with Bao Quoc Thai, priest of the
Diocese of Orange, California.

BOOKS & MEDIA

The Daughters of St. Paul operate book and media centers at the following addresses. Visit, call or write the one nearest you today, or find us on the World Wide Web, www.pauline.org

CALIFORNIA

3908 Sepulveda Blvd, Culver City, CA 90230	310-397-8676
5945 Balboa Avenue, San Diego, CA 92111	858-565-9181
46 Geary Street, San Francisco, CA 94108	415-781-5180

FLORIDA

145 S.W. 107th Avenue, Miami, FL 33174	305-559-6715

HAWAII

1143 Bishop Street, Honolulu, HI 96813	808-521-2731
Neighbor Islands call:	800-259-8463

ILLINOIS

172 North Michigan Avenue, Chicago, IL 60601	312-346-4228

LOUISIANA

4403 Veterans Memorial Blvd, Metairie, LA 70006	504-887-7631

MASSACHUSETTS

885 Providence Hwy, Dedham, MA 02026	781-326-5385

MISSOURI

9804 Watson Road, St. Louis, MO 63126	314-965-3512

NEW JERSEY

561 U.S. Route 1, Wick Plaza, Edison, NJ 08817	732-572-1200

NEW YORK

150 East 52nd Street, New York, NY 10022	212-754-1110
78 Fort Place, Staten Island, NY 10301	718-447-5071

PENNSYLVANIA

9171-A Roosevelt Blvd, Philadelphia, PA 19114	215-676-9494

SOUTH CAROLINA

243 King Street, Charleston, SC 29401	843-577-0175

TENNESSEE

4811 Poplar Avenue, Memphis, TN 38117	901-761-2987

TEXAS

114 Main Plaza, San Antonio, TX 78205	210-224-8101

VIRGINIA

1025 King Street, Alexandria, VA 22314	703-549-3806

CANADA

3022 Dufferin Street, Toronto, ON M6B 3T5	416-781-9131

¡También somos su fuente para libros, videos y música en español!